The Work of
Our Hands

The Work of Our Hands

Faith-Rooted Approaches to
Job Creation, Training, or Placement
In a Context of Concentrated Poverty

Dr. Randy White, editor

The Work of Our Hands
Edited By Randy White

ISBN Print: 978-0-9849618-1-8

Book Layout by Sarah O'Neal | eve custom artwork
Cover photo by Adam Sikora Photography (adamsikora.com),
used by permission.

To order this book, visit
www.condeopress.com

eBook version available on Amazon.com

Printed in the United States of America

Unless otherwise noted, all biblical quotations taken from the
New Revised Standard Version of the Bible, copyright 1989, Division of
Christian Education of the National Council of Churches of Christ in the
United States of America.

We dedicate this publication to the 17% of Fresno's residents who struggle to find or maintain something so central to human dignity: adequate, meaningful employment. May the work of our hands lead to significant work for their hands.

"Let your work be manifest to your servants,

and your glorious power to their children.

Let the favor of the Lord our God be upon us,

and prosper for us the work of our hands—

O prosper the work of our hands!"

Psalm 90:16-17, NRSV

TABLE OF CONTENTS

FOREWORD

By Ashley Swearengin

Our city is making a turnaround, and I see the evidence every day: businesses are growing, schools are improving, and homes and neighborhoods are being rehabilitated. Individuals, churches, and non-profits are now partnering together like never before on the issues that matter the most to our city. *The Work of Our Hands* is a wonderful example of the kind of collaboration our community needs to help bring about citywide transformation.

As Mayor of Fresno, one of my major responsibilities is to draw attention to the most "mission critical" issues in our city, and to do everything possible to direct appropriate resources to address those issues. As you know, local government agencies—the City of Fresno, the County of Fresno, our many schools, and more—simply cannot tackle these issues alone. We must fully engage private citizens and our community partners in helping us move towards a healthy, safe, and productive city.

After working in the field of economic and workforce development for ten years, and now having served as Mayor of Fresno for three years, I can say this with certainty: there is no more "mission critical" issue in our community than adult education—increasing the education and skill levels of those in our adult working population and reducing their barriers to employment. Consider the following statistics:

- An estimated 60,000 adults in Fresno lack a high school diploma or GED certificate. The majority of these adults have children who represent our current generation of students in our local schools.

- According to an article examining California's 2002 birth cohort in *Children and Youth Services Review*, the most significant determining factor of a child's success in school is the education level of his or her parents.

- Despite our city's 15% to 17% unemployment rate, thousands of jobs go unfilled in our area, according to the Fresno Regional Workforce Investment Board, because of the staggering gap between the skills of the people looking for work and the skills required for the available jobs.Nothing is more important for us to address as a community than supporting adults in going back to school and receiving a basic education. In short: education and workforce training lead to employment, employment leads to increased stability at home, and stability at home is the key ingredient to a child's success in school. I believe the way to address the dropout rate in our city is to pursue those who have already dropped out by giving them the encouragement, tools, and opportunities they need to finish their basic education and, in the process, also increase the chances of their own children finishing school.This is what *The Work of Our Hands* is all about, and why it is so important. As this book demonstrates, churches and the faith-rooted non-profit community in Fresno have been helping our city by creating initiatives in adult education, workforce preparation, and job placement.

All across our community, people of faith are showing the kind of "all hands on deck" mentality that is vitally important to the current and future well being of our city. Congregations gathering in places of worship throughout the city have expertise in covering a wide variety of vocations, and that expertise is being put to productive use to provide mentoring programs, job training, job readiness, soft skills training, and much more. I hope we all can see that these actions bring an abundant and lasting hope, not only to particular individuals, but also to our city as a whole.

Because of the efforts of so many, Fresno is leaving the path of chronic, long-term unemployment and economic struggle. I want to encourage our faith-rooted community to continue to place its talents and resources in the service of helping people increase their education and skill levels, which stabilizes and improves their lives, as well as the lives of their children. These are the building blocks of a stronger economy, and the foundation for our city's great turnaround.

Jeremiah 29:7 reminds us to seek the peace of our city—precisely what is described in *The Work of Our Hands*. To those engaged in adult education and job training, mentoring, and employment placement at your places of worship, please know how much your efforts are appreciated and how much they are desperately needed by the thousands of people in our community whom you reach every day. To those of you considering adding this kind of program at your non-profit or place of worship, go for it! Even small efforts will go a long way toward helping our community address this daunting challenge. Imagine this: if every place of worship makes a small effort, think of the collective results we would see across our city!

I am confident about the direction in which we're headed as a city, and I appreciate the vital contributions that our faith-rooted institutions have already made and will continue to make in our community. I wholeheartedly believe that this is our time to experience the turnaround of our city for which so many have hoped, so many have prayed, and so many have worked over the last 20 years. Let's not stop short; let's keep going for it!

BACKGROUND & ACKNOWLEDGEMENTS

This book is the outcome of several key occurrences in Fresno, California. The significant level of concentrated poverty in our region has led to the conclusion by many in the non-profit, business, civic, and faith communities that the status quo is not only morally unacceptable, but dangerous. Low levels of educational attainment and job preparedness mean, among other things, that we cannot attract diversified industry. Recent and repeated employment studies in the Fresno area have shown that thousands of available jobs in our area go unfilled every year because of a "skills gap"—a workforce not prepared to function at required levels[1]. Unless we do something radically different, we will not be able to overcome the soul-killing, economic anemia that has sapped the strength of our people, our city systems, and our social fabric for decades. We must try something new in order to better prepare Fresno's populace for gainful employment.

In January of 2011, Mayor Ashley Swearengin challenged the No Name Fellowship (NNF) to consider what role it might play in enlisting the faith community of Fresno to engage this challenge of preparing people for job creation, training, or placement. This call is consistent with what her taskforce has been saying through the year: "it's time to break through to the next level and reduce and remove remaining barriers that prevent people from accessing the training and education necessary to gain employment."[2]

NNF was launched in 1992 as a coalition of church, non-profit, business, and civic leaders whose purpose was to EXPOSE leaders in Fresno to key challenges facing our city, to EXCHANGE information about these issues, and to help the faith community EMBRACE those issues in significant ways, mobilizing the resources and talents of people of

---

[1] *Learn2Earn*: The Mayor's Adult Education Initiative, supported by the Workforce Investment Board and the Adult Education Taskforce, June 2010, p. 2. (www.Learn2EarnFresno.org)

[2] Ibid., p. 4

faith toward making a difference. NNF has now addressed many issues and mobilized action for 20 years, including the needs of incoming refugee populations, child literacy, teen pregnancy, HIV/AIDS responses, immigration reform, concentrated poverty, gang ministry, and many other issues.

So, for several months, a focus group of the NNF gathered to examine the issue of job readiness, and to research concrete examples of what was working locally, nationally, and internationally. This research group was chaired by Randy White of Bakke Graduate University, and included Kristi Nichols and Bryan Feil (Neighborhood Thrift), Bud Searcy (Fresno Rescue Mission), Artie Padilla (Every Neighborhood Partnership), Chuck Bryant (Good Will Industries), Tamara Glover (FCC-HUD Housing Re-Construction), Sharon Stanley and Alex Castellanos (Fresno Interdenominational Refugee Ministry), Ernesto Escalante (Hogar House), Roger Feenstra (Hope Now for Youth), Paul McLain-Lugowski (Fresno EOC), Jeff Harrington (Highway Cities CDC), and Xavier Garza (Fresno Rescue Mission).

Many people are responsible for the outcome of this project. The international collection of leaders in Bakke Graduate University's doctoral programs contributed examples from their respective contexts. Many gracious churches, businesses and individuals supplied funding for the effort. The Fresno Institute for Urban Leadership also provided meeting space and technical help.

Though as incomplete as the budding movement currently transforming our city, *The Work of Our Hands* is a love offering to the people of Fresno, and a wake-up call to all leaders who seek the well being of the city (Jeremiah 29:7). May God infuse with fruitfulness the work of our hands.

ONE

Why the Church and Christian Non-Profit Agencies in Fresno Should Invest Time, Talent, and Resources Into Job Creation, Job Placement, and Job Readiness Efforts: A Biblical Basis

By Randy White and Sharon Stanley

For many churches, the thought that we should harness the talent and knowledge of the people in the pew and the collective power of the institutional Church toward addressing something as fundamental to life as the need for employment or the mechanisms by which to attain it, is new. We in the Church have often focused more on evangelism, discipleship, and mission, and have let others think about social issues: the causes of poverty, the brokenness of neighborhoods, the unsustainable levels of unemployment, and more. Some Christians have even felt uncomfortable with or suspicious of ministries that engage urban issues, efforts to affect social change, or the confrontation of injustice—wondering if those ministries have somehow left the Gospel behind.

For example, with regard to the issue of employment, many in Christian leadership have simply not acquired the language necessary to link the Christian faith to the human need to work, earn money, and support oneself or one's family. One author notes a revealing survey on this issue: Career Impact Ministries asked around 2,000 Christians the following question: "Have you ever in your life heard a sermon, read a book, listened to a tape, or been to a seminar that applied biblical principles to everyday work issues?" More than 90% answered no.[3]

---

[3] Doug Sherman and William Hendricks, *Your Work Matters to God* (Colorado Springs: Navpress, 1987), 16.

However, over the last few decades, key individuals in what Billy Graham called the "Five Families of the Christian Faith"—Evangelicals, Pentecostals, Mainline Protestants, Catholics, and Orthodox Christians—have steadily embraced a more holistic Gospel, inspired in part by the Lausanne Covenant, Vatican II, The Chicago Declaration, and other documents that have called us to *both* evangelism and social change in the name of Christ. Rev. Dr. John Stott, perhaps the world's most highly regarded evangelical figure, called these two commitments as essential as two wings of a bird, or both sides of a pair of scissors.

In Fresno, this holistic perspective is a non-negotiable. With one of the highest levels of concentrated poverty of any large city in the United States[4] and, at this writing, with 17% unemployment and 43,689 people filing for unemployment benefits[5], as well as a workforce that cannot attract industry due to low educational attainment, we must ask, *How might the church and faith-rooted non-profits of Fresno bring their voices, their passions, their talents, and their resources to the table to address the suffering of a city trapped in an untenable situation?*

LEARNING FROM SCRIPTURE

As Christians, we look to Scripture for guidance in all things. While no verse in the Bible says, "Thou shalt become involved in job creation, placement, or readiness," we have learned to extrapolate principles from the story of Scripture on all sorts of issues—abortion, lifestyle decisions, end-of-life dilemmas, and more—where no simple, direct commands exist to guide us. And while there is no verbatim *prescription*, there is certainly plenty of *description*: biblical precedent and principles laying a foundation for people of faith to be involved.

How does Scripture help us address the catastrophic economic situation we face in Fresno, as well as how employment in general will be a key Kingdom mandate for people of faith in our city? What are some key biblical and theological foundations for the church's involvement?

---

[4] Katrina's Window: Confronting Concentrated Poverty Across America. Brookings Institute , Oct 2005

[5] Learn2Earn, p.4

Here are some places a church, faith-rooted non-profit, or Christian business could start:

1. God's people must commit to establishing *shalom*.

"But seek the shalom of the city to which I have sent you into exile and pray to the Lord on its behalf, for in its shalom you will find your shalom" (Jeremiah 29:7).

Implication: This verse describes the people of God living in Babylon, a city they feared and disliked, yet God called them to seek its *shalom*. A multi-layered word, *shalom* conveys wholeness, integrity, abundance, safety, and peace. According to Old Testament scholar Perry Yoder, it means "making things the way they ought to be—righteous and just—for people, in people, and between people."[6] To philosopher Nicholas Wolterstorff, *shalom* is the "flourishing of all things in their interrelatedness—between us and God, each other, ourselves, and the created order."[7] This is what God's people were commanded to do in Babylon. If we are called to be people of *shalom*, we the Church, scattered in the marketplace and gathered together in strength, must proactively address those forces in our community that undermine *shalom* for the people around us. This includes addressing economic insecurity—a result of various causes, including minimal education, exploitation, a non-diverse economy, few opportunities, and more.

2. God's people must affirm work as good and facilitate its possibility.

"The LORD God took the man and put him in the garden of Eden to till it and to keep it" (Genesis 2:15).

Implication: Here, we learn that, before sin entered the world, God created work for our benefit. In this original, sinless context, we see that God values work and, thus, so should the Church. The creation of work was instrumental, even foundational, as a means by which the

---

[6] Perry Yoder, Shalom: The Bible's Word for Salvation, Justice and Peace (Evangel Press, 1998).

[7] http://www.yale.edu/faith/downloads/Nicholas%20Wolterstorff%20%20-%20God's%20Power%20and%20Human%20Flourishing%202008.pdf, see also *Until Justice and Peace Embrace* (Eerdmans, 1983, second. ed 1994)

human race would honor and glory God through the care and stewardship of His creation. In our fallen state, this makes the necessity of opening doors of employment that much more imperative. In work, God gave humankind a means to continually worship Him, and to exercise the creative gifts granted to each of us. The direct consequence of unemployment is the profound sense of purposelessness and loss of dignity. The deeper spiritual consequence of unemployment, even underemployment, is the issue—realized or not—that an individual isn't achieving his or her purpose in life.

3. God's people must live out a commitment to work as a sacred expression and gift of the Holy Spirit, and help all people experience it.

"See, I have called by name Bezalel son of Uri son of Hur, of the tribe of Judah: and I have filled him with divine spirit, with ability, intelligence, and knowledge in every kind of craft, to devise artistic designs, to work in gold, silver, and bronze, in cutting stones for setting, and in carving wood, in every kind of craft. Moreover, I have appointed with him Oholiab son of Ahisamach, of the tribe of Dan; and I have given skill to all the skillful, so they may make all that I have commanded you" (Exodus 31:2-6).

Implication: Work, skills for work, the creative process, and production—these are all Holy Spirit activities. It is appropriate and necessary that the Church cooperate with the initiative of God's Spirit in the facilitation of people's ability to work. Unfortunately, however, this hasn't always been the Church's posture. We need to better understand how faith impacts every aspect of life, and to see work as one way of living out God's purpose for us. If there are whole segments of people in a city unable to participate in the blessings and dignity of work, this is an indicator that things are not right according to God's plan. In addition, Deuteronomy 15:4 says, "There will, however, be no one in need among you, because the LORD is sure to bless you in the land that the LORD your God is giving you as a possession to occupy."

4. God's people must value workers.

"Then God said, 'Let us make humankind in our image, according to

our likeness . . . So God created humankind in his image, in the image of God he created them; male and female he created them" (Genesis 1:26-27).

"You have given them dominion over the works of your hands; you have put all things under their feet" (Psalm 8:6).

Implication: God is a worker—God made things—and we, as people made in His image, are called to "express something of who He is and what he wants done in the world."[8] All people deserve this opportunity. The Church must feature and support an ethic that values workers and that holds them up as image bearers of God in the world, in addition to helping parishioners find their place in that process.

5. God's people must contribute to a new vision of society, one that reflects the new heavens and new earth as described in Scripture.

"I am creating a new heavens and a new earth; everything of the past will be forgotten. Celebrate and be glad forever! I am creating a Jerusalem full of happy people. I will celebrate with Jerusalem and all of its people; there will be no more crying or sorrow in that city. No child will die in infancy; everyone will live to a ripe old age. Anyone a hundred years old will be considered young and to die younger than that will be considered a curse. My people will live in the houses they build; they will enjoy grapes from their own vineyards. No one will take away their homes or vineyards. My chosen people will live to be as old as trees, and they will enjoy what they have earned. Their work won't be wasted and their children won't die of dreadful diseases" (Isaiah 65:17-23, Contemporary English Version).

Implication: God is inviting us into His vision of a new society that He will create and is, even now, creating. This passage addresses the often calamitous circumstances faced by people in poor neighborhoods: houses that do not belong to their occupants, regular evictions, early infant death due to addictions or poor health access, a lack of sufficient earnings, or wasted work. We as God's people can participate in previews of the city to come, employing the values we see represented in God's ultimate goal.

---

[8] Word in Life Bible, Thomas Nelson Publishers, p 783.

6. God's people must utilize communities and small businesses in solving economic problems.

"Now the wife of a member of the company of prophets cried to Elisha, 'Your servant my husband is dead; and you know that your servant feared the LORD, but a creditor has come to take my two children as slaves.' Elisha said to her, 'What shall I do for you? Tell me, what do you have in the house?' She answered, 'Your servant has nothing in the house, except a jar of oil.' He said, 'Go outside, borrow vessels from all your neighbors, empty vessels and not just a few. Then go in, and shut the door behind you and your children, and start pouring into all these vessels; when each is full, set it aside.' So she left him and shut the door behind her and her children; they kept bringing vessels to her, and she kept pouring. When the vessels were full, she said to her son, 'Bring me another vessel.' But he said to her, 'There are no more.' Then the oil stopped flowing. She came and told the man of God, and he said, 'Go sell the oil and pay your debts, and you and your children can live on the rest" (2 Kings 4:1-7).

Implication: These verses show us that God used his leader (Elisha), and the community who provided the jars, and the meager resources of the woman herself (oil), and the involvement and energy of her own family, and His divine power to meet this woman's need. Yet, God's intervention didn't stop there. The solution provided was enough to create a cottage industry and/or small business for the woman—a job to meet her family's needs. The more than 500 churches in Fresno could be creatively equipped to do the same with those who face barriers to employment.

These brief encounters with key passages from Scripture help us begin to glimpse the ways in which work is essential to our dignity and identity, as well as a means to meet need.

THINKING THROUGH THE LENS OF GOD'S IDENTITY

Another way to think theologically about this issue is through the lens of God's identity. According to author Larry Peabody[9]—who compiled

---

[9] Larry Peabody, personal comments, July 10, 2011. Peabody is the author of Serving Christ in the Workplace: Secular Work is Full Time Service (CLC Ministries, 2004), and Job Shadowing Daniel (Outskirts Pres, 2010).

thoughts specifically for us in Fresno—we the Church ought to speak to and be involved in work or employment-related issues *because of who God is*. This Trinitarian approach is articulated as follows:

God is Creator, who made us in His likeness to create—under His authority, and to "rule over all the earth" (Genesis 1:26-27). We do so through our work in all of its various forms. **Implication**: The Church leads the way in a creative approach to the challenges of employment in our city because God initially modeled this posture for us.

God is Sustainer, who, through His Spirit, maintains and provides for His creation (Psalm 104:14). Through our work, God provides and cares for people, animals, plants, and the earth itself. **Implication**: The Church fosters a subculture of work known for its care in all those realms because it reflects the second person of the Trinity.

God is Redeemer, who, through his Son, saves us from sin and death. In our work—both word and deed—God calls us to carry out His redemptive work worldwide: buying back broken systems—including economic and class systems—that make a sustainable livelihood impossible (Colossians 3:17; Titus 2:10). **Implication**: Redemptive work goes beyond individuals to include systems, even systems of livelihood. The Church demonstrates that Jesus is powerful enough to transform even these.

God is Consummator, who will bring all things under His own benevolent rule. Our work is to contribute to that ultimate end. Even then, our work will involve co-ruling with Him (2 Timothy 2:12; Revelation 20:6). **Implication**: The Church creates a preview of that Kingdom—which is here now, but not yet in its fullness—when we contribute to just systems, meet human needs, and provide people with the dignity of work.

The implication of seeing the issue of work and employment through the lens of God's identity and consummated reign is that the Church *scattered* is as crucial to the Kingdom of God as is the Church *gathered*. However, so much of our experience of the Church is organized around our gathered life alone. It is appropriate that we equip our churches to assist all of God's people in living out the call to work. It makes sense that we would address barriers in people's lives that prevent them from responding to this call.

WHAT DOES LOVE REQUIRE OF US?

We have seen key passages from Scripture that set a foundation for our involvement in something as basic as employment, and we have understood that God's identity calls us to follow His creative, redemptive, and sustaining work. Yet, what might still help us round out the picture? Perhaps the greatest thing yet: love.

Love is the mother of all themes in the Bible. So, how might this provide a lens for us as we think about the Church's involvement in helping people stabilize their economic lives, or prepare more effectively for employment? Author Neal Johnson helps us here, with comments particularly crafted for Fresno[10]:

> Job readiness training and economic development are designed to help people in distress with the very real problem of supporting themselves and their families. They address individuals and their specific needs, but through a systemic, community-wide effort to create a healthier, vibrant, and meaningful life for an entire community. Unemployment is an economic issue that must be met head-on to help people survive. It is also so much more than that, as you all in Fresno are so acutely aware. Having a job is not just having a paycheck. It is the key to restoring a person's self-esteem, their sense of worth, their dignity, their place in society, and their commitment to the health and stability of the community.
>
> Helping people be qualified for a job, and then to find and keep that job, is of monumental importance to every community, especially those with the particular challenges of Fresno. This is true not just morally and economically, but practically: many major social issues that are directly correlated to a community's action or inaction in the area of job creation.[11] The following biblical themes give insight to this:

---

[10] C Neal Johnson personal comments for Fresno leaders, July 11, 2011

[11] *Business as Mission: A Comprehensive Guide to Theory and Practice* by C. Neal Johnson (InterVarsity, 2009 - See pp. 34-50, especially 34-37 for a focused discussion of this point.)

1. John 13:34-35: Jesus told His disciples: "I give you a new commandment, that you love one another. Just as I have loved you, you also should love one another. By this everyone will know that you are my disciples, if you have love for one another." **Implication**: Love is an action. True love cannot ignore the most basic human need: people must work to provide for their lives and families. Providing the means to work is an act of love.

2. Ephesians 5:1, 25: Scripture calls us to "be imitators of God, as beloved children, and live in love, as Christ loved us and gave himself up for us, a fragrant offering and sacrifice to God . . . Husbands, love your wives, just as Christ loved the church and gave himself up for her." Scripture also illustrates in countless ways that Jesus loved us—and He did so holistically. The list of Jesus' holistic, healing miracles testifies to who He was, but it also testifies to His compassion and commitment to help people with their temporal pain, not just their eternal destiny. **Implication**: Walking in a holistic love towards a person means being committed to those things that most practically impact their life. Will the Church be known for this brand of love, or only something less tangible?

3. Matthew 11:3-5: Jesus answered John the Baptist's inquiry as to whether He was the promised Messiah by replying that John would know who He was by what He has done: "'Go and tell John what you hear and see: the blind receive their sight, the lame walk, the lepers are cleansed, the deaf hear, the dead are raised, and the poor have good news brought to them.'" **Implication**: Will the Church pursue the same agenda as Jesus did, even if it means getting involved with those with special needs, those needing health care, those marginalized to the fringes, and more—all those in Jesus' society who would have been difficult to employ?

4. Luke 10:25-37: In the Parable of the Good Samaritan, Jesus explains how we are to deal with those in need. The Samaritan lifted the waylaid traveler out of the mud; took him to a place of safety, peace, and rest; bandaged his wounds; fed and cared for him; and paid for it all. Then Jesus told his audience, "Go and do likewise." **Implication**: Involvement in things that are messy, things that are the problems of others, things that cost us money, and things that have no guaranteed payback are normative for the Church.

5. Mark 12:29-31: When asked which of God's commandments was the most important, Jesus responded, "'The first is, 'Hear, O Israel: the Lord our God, the Lord is one; you shall love the Lord your God with all your heart, and with all your soul, and with all your strength. The second is, 'You shall love your neighbor as yourself.' There is no other commandment greater than these.'" **Implication**: Here, the message is simple: love God and love people. How do we best love people? By meeting their *real* needs in the name and love of Jesus. One of humanity's major needs for each person to support his or herself and his or her family. This requires an income, which comes from a job, which is dependent on the economic health of a community. Accordingly, we love God and love people when we help them meet life's basic, economic needs.

6. Matthew 25:31-46: In the Parable of the Goats and the Sheep, Jesus dispels any doubts that loving others as stated above is not integral to following Him. This parable makes several key points with regard to the issue at hand, one which cannot be ignored by the Church or any believing Christian: on Judgment Day, we will be held accountable for how we dealt with the hungry, the thirsty, the homeless, the stranger, the naked, the sick, and the imprisoned. **Implication**: All of these conditions are tragic, direct economic consequences of not having a way to earn a living. Jesus tells us that how we deal with those in economic need and/or distress will be a sign of whether we are truly His followers.

This input from Neal Johnson helps us ask some key questions of ourselves:

1. From the Luke 10 Parable of the Good Samaritan, we learn to ask: *Does Jesus' command to "go and do likewise" include*

reaching out to people whose lack of educational success has trapped them in work situations where they are being injured by bosses who take advantage of their lack of options?

2. From the Mark 12 passage about loving God and loving our neighbors as ourselves, we learn to ask: *If we love ourselves by ensuring that we have a livelihood, should we not contribute to loving our neighbors in the same way?*

3. From the Matthew 25 Parable of the Goats and the Sheep, we learn to ask: *To what extent do we connect own well being to the well being of everyone in our community who wants to work?*

STORIES FROM FRESNO

Before we make the mistake of operating from theory or principle alone, we must also choose to look at this issue through the lens of experience and story.

Faith-rooted job readiness ministries recognize God as Creator, the source of all that is. God's creative activity is not limited to some remote past. Rather, our God—who will create a "new heaven and new earth" (Revelation 21:1)—is constantly initiating new possibilities, new beginnings, and new experiences. These new possibilities are personal—they deal with our days and nights. They occur in the realm of our real and daily lives, for our God who "knit me together in my mother's womb" (Psalm 139:13-14) is creatively at work throughout our lives as we seek new beginnings. This applies especially in something as basic as our need to work, which is why we come back time and time again to this truth: *Job creation efforts are inseparably tied with God's work as Creator, who authors all possibilities.*

For example, take Vanna, a former member of an Asian gang in Fresno. For him, this principle meant God's people creating a ministry (Hope Now for Youth) that would reach out to him by providing a job, mentoring him to learn skills that would sustain him in that job, and the friendship of a positive, Christian male role model who would walk with him in his transition to a responsible, productive life. Vanna would eventually go on staff with that agency and work for a decade placing hundreds of young men from similar backgrounds into full-time employment, getting them off the streets and into new, God-inspired opportunities for a life of blessing. Vanna also went onto college and then seminary, where he finished a master's degree. God used Hope Now for Youth, with all of its specialized expertise, to create something new and beautiful.

As we recognize the Creator's desire to be at work within something as basic as our human need for daily work, we celebrate God's desire for partnership with us. We have no separate reality from God, for we were created "in the image of God" (Genesis 1:26). We are dependant upon God; yet we recognize God has something for us to do in the world! Stamped by God's identity, we have been given strength and have been commanded to be fruitful (Genesis 1:28). *Therefore, faith-rooted efforts at creating jobs or training people for job placement must seek to "call out" and celebrate God's desire for fruitfulness within every human being. We do not rest from this effort until all can participate in the blessing of a fruitful life.*

Joe D. came to the Fresno Interdenominational Refugee Ministry (FIRM) many years ago when he was just getting off parole. We all know how it is significantly more difficult for someone with a record to get decent work, even if he or she has experienced true conversion, as Joe had. Everyone came to experience Joe as being the guy who goes above and beyond what is asked of him. You ask him to pick up supplies once, and he'll be your guy from now on. You need someone to lead music for your church, "I've never done that, but I can try." Joe always had things to keep him busy. One morning, Joe came into the FIRM office because he had lost his job of several years. With his background of being an ex-parolee and in an economy where jobs were disappearing, things looked rough. Even for someone as resourceful as Joe, things felt bleak. However, from that first meeting, Joe faithfully and repeatedly returned to the office, each time with new applications to apply for new jobs. He always arrived at FIRM with optimism that this was going to be the week he would find a job. His faith was never shaken, and he was never deterred from his goal to continue being self-sustaining. When all of the leads seemed to be exhausted, the Lord finally opened up a great opportunity for Joe: he was able to find a job with an employment agency and began working in Kingsburg, California. Though he knows that this job came from the Lord, he knows he is called to continue in this path and pursue even greater opportunities. He had come to experience his God-inspired potential from this new job, and it was better than anything he ever had in his former way of life.

Taking hold of this new potential is more difficult than some might imagine. The struggles of poverty, lack of English, transportation challenges, family issues, and daily realities of poor neighborhoods fight against it. Simply knowing what your potential is can be a challenge for the vulnerable. Even Moses, who had lost his privileged place in life, was intimidated by the task the Lord set before him (Exodus 4:10). Mary also struggled to comprehend the incomprehensible as the Lord announced her overwhelming assignment, asking, "How can this be, since I am a virgin?" (Luke 1:34).

These images reveal God's promise of faithfulness and the Holy Spirit to empower all of us—especially the vulnerable among us. The Church can be a vehicle of this message to those in our community who exist in the shadows and on the margins. We can find creative ways of being in relationship with those who struggle to find work, encouraging them to "Be strong and bold, have no fear or dread . . . it is the LORD your God who goes with you; he will never fail you or forsake you" (Deuteronomy 31:6). Efforts by the people of God in our city endeavor to build up the most vulnerable of us to have the needed courage for the often overwhelming task of getting ready to work, and to take hold of "a life worthy of the calling to which [they] have been called" (Ephesians 4:1).

Tout Tou Bounthapanya of FIRM tells the story of Somboun, a Lao woman who came to the ministry for help. Somboun said that she thanks God so much for FIRM and for the employees at FIRM who helped her prepare a suitable resume, fill out application forms, provide transportation to job opportunities, and connect her to potential employers. Eventually, she was hired by Community Hospital and worked there for a while, until necessary surgery made the job impossible. These days, she works as a house cleaner. She said that before she came to know Christ, she didn't know how to thank God for the good things in life. She now has faith in God and she credits FIRM. She says, "God gave me strength and I don't give up." It's not easy, but she's doing her best.

During the time that she didn't have a job, Somboun also helped family members and relatives with their English, in order to help them prepare for work, as well. She also has four children to care for, but she has the spirit of work in her. She says, "God is always giving me the chance to help people in many different ways every day." God used the specialized expertise of FIRM's Jobs First program to help Somboun take hold of her potential.

CONCLUSION

When God outlines the instructions for His people in setting up their new identity as followers of Yahweh, He said, that there will "be no one in need among you" (Deuteronomy 15:4). However, as it it turns out, the Hebrew in that verse is uncertain. Is God being *prescriptive*, issuing a command that the society should be ordered in a way that all who can work will be able to and, thus, avoiding societal poverty? Or is He being *descriptive*, saying that if you set up your society correctly, the outcome will be that there is economic opportunity and, therefore, no systemic poverty? Either way, God has envisioned us being proactive in seeing that economic justice is normative. Does Jesus' statement that "You always have the poor with you" (Mark 14:7) negate God's vision for a just society in early Israel? Is he acquiescing to the reality of poverty and giving up on the dream that Israel or the Church will be a contributor to an economically just system? No. In fact, the second half of that sentence, which often fails to get quoted, encourages us to "do good to them ..." (Mark 14:7) as does the Deut. 15 passage. And, we see from the earliest example of those in leadership within the Church that they had to be proactive in dealing with the issue of economic injustice and providing for the care of the Hellenistic widows who had been cut out of the distribution food during the famine (Acts 6).

This chapter has only scratched the surface of how Scripture provides a solid foundation for the Church—both scattered and gathered—being involved in ministries of job creation, readiness, or placement. Even from this short reflection, we take encouragement that God's people can play a vital role in helping their city become all that God intends. Scripture assures us that "When it goes well with the righteous, the city rejoices" (Proverbs 11:10). What about those who struggle to be employable as a result of educational failure? What about those who, in their conversion, hope for a second chance after the mistakes of their youth? What about those who, through some disability, are stuck in minimum wage jobs? Will the day come when we see *them* as the righteous of that verse? When they prosper, so will the whole city.

"But seek the [shalom] of the city where I have sent you into exile, and pray to the LORD on its behalf, for in its [shalom] you will find your [shalom]" (Jeremiah 29:7).

TWO

The Art of the Possible:
Noteworthy National & International Examples of Faith-Rooted
Job Creation, Job Training, or Job Placement

By Kristi Nichols

It may come as a great surprise to many that churches and faith-rooted organizations throughout our country and world have been innovatively applying the biblical strategy of serving with the love of Christ by addressing the challenges of unemployment. We have been so encouraged to learn of these models, and we feel we can learn much from those who have made concrete efforts and are currently having an impact.

We have gathered handfuls of great examples, but, before we explore them, let's keep our focus on people by telling a real story emerging from a wonderful model called Christ Kitchen in Spokane, Washington. This story gives us a glimpse into how God is making all things new and rebuilding lives by means of work.

We'll call this woman Arianna. She writes:

> Awaiting release from prison, I remember thinking, "How will I be able to support my family with a criminal record? No one will hire me; what will I do?" That was five years ago. I heard . . . that Christ Kitchen is a place where I could make a little cigarette money. So, I came for that reason. But then I sat through the Bible studies and was intrigued. The Bible study focused on Jesus, explained the Bible, and related my life to Scripture. I wanted to hear more about this guy Jesus. I've learned that He is a loving, forgiving God. I have learned to love

myself and my family, and I feel blessed through my job. It's been like a rebirth. Now, I use prayer instead of withdrawing and turning to drugs. I was shocked when I was asked to become a manager. They told me I was a good, hard worker, but that was hard to understand because I felt so dirty and unworthy coming out of prison. I felt so blessed to be considered for a higher position and to be given an additional opportunity. Now I am working full-time . . . I'm learning to be an obedient servant so that God's love and mercy can freely flow through me to the people around me.

As someone motivated by a deep love for pastoral and cross-cultural ministry, I never intended to find my calling in a small business. However, as I transitioned from being an inner-city missionary to stay-at-home mom, I was at a loss for how to build relationships with others outside of my immediate social circle. So, it was a strategic step to begin volunteering at Neighborhood Thrift Store in Fresno. It became a daily opportunity to work alongside people who often came from vulnerable situations in an environment where relationships and sharing faith in Christ are encouraged. The initial months of volunteering compelled me to develop an understanding, passion, and vision for the "business as mission" model of ministry.

Now, as the Work Experience Coordinator at Neighborhood Thrift, I experience how the Church engaging in job creation, relationships, and job readiness is a powerful witness to God's creative compassion for one of our region's greatest concerns: unemployment. We have seen in the past few decades that the Church in the Fresno area has the God-given capacity to effectively utilize its resources to be a witness of Christ's love by creating solutions to challenging problems. Now is the time for the Church in the Fresno area to further extend our witness into the realm of employment and employability. Our research has found numerous models— in the Fresno area, throughout the country, and internationally—of how engaging people in the context of work has a ripple effect of transforming individuals and families to become "self-sufficient and Christ-dependent."[12] The models listed in this chapter are

---

[12] www.christkitchen.org

faith-rooted organizations. However, we have included in the Appendix other non-profit organizations because of their effectiveness in helping create jobs and assist people in improving their job readiness.

WHAT WE LEARNED

Regardless of variations, we've discovered a few crucial elements common to each of these successful organizations. No matter what any particular job creation or job training strategy a church or faith-rooted non-profit chooses, these elements should be incorporated:

Context: Successful models serve as a context for people to engage with others who care. They also serve as a context for exposure to knowledge, for the opportunity to apply that knowledge, and for making connections to equip people for change. Many felt it was important to first set your vision and then to link the specifics of your effort to the calling and leadership qualities of robust leadership—either your own, or of those in your institution.

Accessibility: While the face of unemployment has become more varied in recent years, those with barriers to employment need an accessible entry point. Successful models are accessible in that a person can step into a program "as is" and with only a willingness to try.

Basic Job Skills: Successful models offer education, and some even provide opportunities to put into practice the basic skills of getting a job (i.e., resume writing, interviewing, Internet job searching, etc.) and of job retention (i.e., attendance, work ethic, conflict resolution, etc.).

Demographic Specificity: Successful models focus on a specific city or neighborhood, and, often, a particular people group.

Process-Oriented: Process-oriented programs allow people the time and support needed to learn and develop. Successful models aim to be a transition step to long-term, permanent employment with another employer.

Multi-Faceted Service: Successful models recognize the multi-faceted challenges some participants face in becoming self-sufficient.

In addition to job readiness, these models equip job seekers by offering relational services such as mentoring and counseling, practical services like computer labs and tattoo removal, and faith-building services such as Bible study and connections to churches.

Longevity: Successful models are sustainable for years and have the longevity to not only hone their people-oriented practices, but—for those that create jobs—to also grow and maintain a profit-making business. For some models, longevity includes the financial support of donors, yet most report that the majority of their annual budgets are financed through their businesses.

Networks and Partnerships: Successful models have required networks and partnerships with individuals, churches, businesses, and/or other organizations.

Christ as the Foundation: Successful models readily recognize that a life reconciled to God through Christ causes and sustains transformation (Colossians 1:19-20). Creating jobs and improving employability is the Church pursuing reconciliation: putting things back into right relationship—Christ's love in action. Reconciling people to God and engaging in His transforming process, not just finding people a job, is the mission of these organizations.[13]

NOTEWORTHY EXAMPLES

Advance Memphis

Memphis, Tennessee
www.advancememphis.org

Advance Memphis, founded in 1999, aims to serve adults in inner-city Memphis "by empowering residents to acquire knowledge, resources, and skills to be economically self-sufficient through the gospel of Jesus Christ." Program opportunities include Jobs For Life classes (required as the initial phase), GED preparation classes, Financial Freedom classes, and hands-on training and classroom instruction for certification

---

[13] Steve Corbett and Brian Fikkert, *When Helping Hurts*, Moody Publishers, 2009.

in forklift and warehouse skills. In addition, some graduates of the classes are given the opportunity for paid employment and "real world" experience in the Advance Memphis Outsourcing Program, or are referred to Advance Memphis Staffing for employment opportunities with one of Advance Memphis' business partners.

Unique to Advance Memphis is its Individual Development Account Program. This savings program for graduates of the Financial Freedom classes earns $2 for every $1 they deposit into their savings accounts. This encourages the habit of saving and greatly increases an individual's financial net worth.

Advance Memphis' staff members point to the volunteer mentor relationships as a key component to a participant's development. When participants begin with Advance Memphis in the first phase of a Jobs For Life class, they join a weekly small group lead by a volunteer mentor. As the participants engage in various other opportunities, the mentor continues to provide support. Advance Memphis tells of a woman who had recently completed her GED, after seven prior attempts, before coming to Advance Memphis. The woman attributes finally achieving success because of the encouragement and support she received from her mentor.

Advent Ministries and Advent Industries

Elyira, Ohio
www.adventtoday.org and www.adventworks.com

For the last 30 years, Advent Ministries has been "quietly about the business of changing lives" through hands-on, paid job training, job placement, and a holistic approach to ministering to individuals through spiritual, emotional, social, and educational development. The organization collaborates with various service organizations and churches, and provides instruction and training for inmates in the county corrections systems. Ed Seabold, one of the founders, states, "Our primary purpose is to hire people, not because of how serious their background is, but how willing they are to make a change and be productive." Advent Ministries has served over 1,000 people, with an estimated 90% in regular employment. The ministry is currently reorganizing.

In 2010, Advent Industries began a new business: building and selling bunk beds. The beds sell at affordable, retail prices, yet they encourage donors to sponsor a family by donating $285. These donations enable Advent Industries to provide bunk beds for the children of low-income families.

Agape Christian Worship Center Businesses

Albany, Georgia
www.agapealbany.org

Agape Moving Services (www.movinghelp.com/agapemovingservices) is a moving labor help service that supports U-Haul and other customers with loading and unloading their moving trucks or vans. In addition, they provide residential packing and unpacking, and include cleaning services.

Just Jump Event Rental (www.justjumprental.com) is an inflatable party rental business that rents inflatable bounce houses, popcorn and cotton candy machines, and other party-related entertainment to customers for birthday parties, special events, family reunions, and more.Both businesses started in 2011 and have grown steadily. They currently have six employees on a part-time, per order basis. Workers have opportunities to work both businesses, and both are profitable. Initially, the concern was whether or not these ventures would be sustainable. These days, however, they are going well. Their mission is economic empowerment for the Church, as well as job creation. The Gospel is also a key component, and routine opportunities exist for personal evangelism, as well as the discipling that takes place as workers drive with team leaders to the job sites. Church leaders volunteer time to manage job requests and workers. Leaders also promote the business through word of mouth. Agape Christian Worship Center also plays a vital role in screening candidates for employment.

An Anonymous Restaurant (anonymous for the purpose of security)

India

The restaurant was created as a for-profit business for the purpose of multiplying donor investments to share with local area ministries. The restaurant was started with a capital investment of $300,000, which purchased a 4,000-square-foot building and all that was required to outfit it with the necessary fixtures and supplies to start a restaurant.

The money was entirely raised by donations in $100 dollar increments, as an investment in the restaurant. However, the return is not for the personal profit of the donors. For example, if a donor gave $1,000, then that donor purchased 10 units of the restaurant. It was then up to the donor to assign his or her 10 units, in the allotments of his or her choice, to any of the 17 ministries that serve in the same city as the restaurant. The units are paid out to the ministries on a monthly basis from the profit of the restaurant after the monthly costs, including wages, of the restaurant have been paid.

The ministry focus of the restaurant is to reach out through relationships to the employees (an average of 40), to the multiple vendors that supply the restaurant, and to the customers.

Belay Enterprises

Denver, Colorado
www.belay.org

Launched in 1995 as a collaborative effort between business owners, builders, pastors, and leaders, Belay Enterprises aims to "partner with area churches to develop businesses to employ and job-train individuals rebuilding lives from addiction, homelessness, prison, and/or poverty, in order to strengthen families and neighborhoods." Essential to living out the mission is not only Belay's contribution to economic development, but also its offer of personal support to individuals employees, functioning as a "strong partner" and a "safety-net" for those becoming empowered and "set free from the past."

Businesses started by Belay Enterprises include BUD'S (Building Unity and Dignity through Service) Warehouse, a home improvement thrift store; Baby Bud's, a thrift store focused on employing low-income, single mothers; Freedom Cleaning Services; Good Neighbor Garage, a mechanic garage that repairs donated cars and resells them at affordable prices to low-income families in need of transportation; New Beginnings Custom Woodwork; and Purple Door

Coffee (still in development), an effort to employ homeless youth.

To multiply its efforts beyond the capacity of Belay Enterprises, the organization launched The Ascent Venture Fund in 2003, which provides "low-interest micro loans to community-based businesses that create jobs in their neighborhoods." In addition to funding, The Ascent Venture Fund recruits business leaders to "identify, launch, and provide mentor support of promising new ventures."

Rachel, a graduate of BUD'S Warehouse now works at a regular job in the community, and has the goal of working as an ambulance driver. In sharing about her experience at BUD'S Warehouse, she explains that, when she started, she was just coming off drugs and out of prison, and totally dependent on government assistance. However, she gained a sense of self-worth and confidence by working alongside others in a "positive, Christian environment." And, shortly after starting at BUD'S, Rachel met her primary goal of regaining custody of her daughter.

Boaz and Ruth RestorCorps

Richmond, Virginia
www.boazandruth.com

The story of Boaz and Ruth RestorCorps begins with a concern for the disparity of wealth and resources in Richmond, and was envisioned by Martha Rollins, the owner of an antiques shop. She shared her vision with a "women's roundtable" and those women joined her in the plan. One friend offered the use of a vacant building she owned in an impoverished Richmond neighborhood, another offered a $150,000 grant matched by a church, and a third donated her household of valuable furniture to be resold. These resources began the first of now six Boaz and Ruth businesses, which function as tools and contexts for "restoring lives and communities through relationships."

Since its beginning in 2002, Boaz and Ruth RestoreCorps has come to include several people on staff. They write, "A mighty river never comes into existence by itself, but is the result of many streams coming together into one strong body. So it is with Boaz and Ruth. While Martha Rollins was building (her antique shop), Rosa Jiggets was selling food out of a bus and praying . . . Ellen Robertson was becoming politically active and Lloyd Price was following God's call to return to Highland Park. Clarence and Veronica (the first employees) were living their lives, not knowing that they were waiting for Boaz and Ruth, and the . . . Customer was developing the means and resources that would be needed. All came together in good time—God's time. Boaz and Ruth is not the story of any one person, it's the story of many people coming together out of the faith and loving concern for people in their city."

Boaz and Ruth serves the purposes of providing life and work skills through employment in its businesses, re-entry assistance for released prisoners, and "commercial revitalization for the troubled community of Highland Park" and other "culturally and economically disparate communities within the Richmond metropolitan area."

Cafe Sonshine and Higher Ground Landscaping

Detroit, Michigan
www.centraldetroitchristian.org

Businesses of the Central Detroit Christian Community Development Corporation, both Cafe Sonshine and Higher Ground Landscaping are considered "simple but ambitious" businesses. They employ "hard to employ" local residents, providing them with an opportunity to work and earn a wage. Cafe Sonshine, a family-style restaurant in a Detroit neighborhood, employs teens and young adults and has built a customer base by serving good tasting, healthy food at inexpensive prices. Higher Ground Landscaping, a yard service business, started as two men cutting lawns and has now grown into a crew of eight skilled landscapers with a growing list of clients.

Career Actions Ministry, Menlo Park Presbyterian Church

Menlo Park, California
www.mppc.org/calendar/career-actions-ministry

Eastside Take Control, an Ecumenical Career Network Group

Detroit, Michigan

Both of these laity-lead ministries offer compassionate and practical responses to the concerns of the unemployed in their respective communities. Among the large number of our country's unemployed are individuals for whom employment had been relatively accessible prior to the economic recession. However, these individuals now face a job search process that has dramatically changed over the years and, as such, is extremely competitive. These ministries to reach out to their congregations, as well as the "un-churched" in their communities through seminars regarding employment issues; classes and consulting for computer skills; resume and interview upgrades; Internet network groups; and small groups for encouragement, prayer, Scripture reading, and accountability. These ministries also serve by facilitating connections between job seekers and employers.

These ministries also focus on the need to provide a context that keeps people engaged socially and provides accountability to not give up their job search. The provision for emotional and spiritual support is a vital part of how they serve their communities. One participant reported to *Christianity Today* ("Blessed are the Jobless," January 2012) that her six months of unemployment were "scarring," largely due to the response of former coworkers, as well as the lack of support. Steve Murata of Career Actions Ministry reports in the same article: "It lifts their spirits. They understand that there is a framework or organization that can provide some of the emotional and spiritual pieces that are missing from secular job-seeking aid." Ben Van Arragon of Eastside Take Control states that "what often stands in the way for people . . . is how they feel about themselves and their job loss." These ministries speak biblical truth, teaching for not just a season of unemployment, but for life.

Eastside Take Control is a joint ministry of six churches—ecumenical in that they are not all from the same denomination. Each church had a vision for a support ministry for job seekers, and each realized the greater potential if they worked together. They have found that the ecumenical nature of the ministry has been especially attractive to those outside the church community, as they sense that the unified outreach effort is an authentic commitment to serve. Ben Van Arragon describes the experience of working side by side with other churches as enriching.

Christ Kitchen

Spokane, Washington
www.christkitchen.org

Christ Kitchen opened its doors in 1998 with the mission of "providing work, instruction, discipleship, support, and fellowship for women living in poverty . . . [enabling] women to learn to work, to become employable, and, eventually, to support themselves and their families without reliance on government programs or destructive relationships." The inspiration for Christ Kitchen evolved for founder and director Jan Martinez as she sought an effective strategy to connect patients into group therapy and Bible study, while working as a therapist in the healthcare field at Christ Clinic. "Assuming that money would be an incentive for impoverished women to meet together in a Christ-centered mission, the idea for a job training project was conceived." The original job training project of two women making soup mixes and meeting for discipleship has grown into a micro business that employs 36 women per year and produces dried mixes, gift baskets, catered meals, and a restaurant-style deli.

With the help of volunteer mentors—who not only meet one-on-one with participants, but also work alongside employees—individual attention is given to help employees deal with life issues that prevent successfully handling a job. The primary goal of Christ Kitchen is for women to become "self-sufficient and Christ-dependent." Time and effort are given to the process of growth and development at Christ Kitchen, knowing that, without them, there is a chance that destructive habits will return and cause failure at a future job.

Enterprise International, a division of Church Resource Ministries

Anaheim, California
www.enterpriseinternational.org

"The place where you get to DO business for Christ," Enterprise International believes God is at work in the business community, inspiring and empowering that community to share its resources and expertise with communities in need in the United States and throughout the world.

The primary purpose of Church Resource Ministries is empowering individuals and communities for Christian leadership development. The concept for a small business being a viable context for leadership development began in the early 1990s in post-communist Romania. The need for employment, and the lacking work ethic due to the effects of communism, inspired a successful businessman from Orange County to start a small business in Iasi. With the successes in Romania, the concept has grown into Enterprise International.

Enterprise International develops highly contextualized, empowerment-focused businesses in the United States, as well as in various other countries and contexts. In Los Angeles, a missionary mentoring inner-city youth was met with the challenge of helping the youth stay in college, as they were pressured by their parents to contribute to the family income and, as such, unable to pay for textbooks. Enterprise International came alongside these students and resourced them to begin an online bookstore, which now provides them with income, as well as creating a context for their ongoing development, not only as employees, but also as business partners (La IC Book Collective on Facebook). Since the inception of the online bookstore, other neighbors in the Los Angeles community have been resourced through Enterprise International to begin an online store, selling global goods produced by international, micro-businesses.

However, whether located in Los Angeles or elsewhere in the world, all Enterprise International businesses not only empower through economic and leadership development, but they also have the additional purpose of funding local ministries. The businesses are for-profit, with the commitment of using a portion of their profits to support the ministries of others.

FaithWorks of Abilene

Abilene, Texas
www.faithworksofabiline.org

Since its inception in 2003, FaithWorks of Abilene has kept to its mission of helping the underemployed—through personal, career, academic, and spiritual development—acquire the confidence and skills necessary for gainful employment. This statement includes the fact that, while FaithWorks addresses basic employment skills, it does not neglect the other requirements for successful long-term careers. Those "soft skills" include self-confidence, a strong work ethic, a greater understanding of what employers desire in an employee, and the need for stability. Faith-Works also seeks to address and remove all barriers to financial stability for its students, whether personal, spiritual, or academic. In addition, FaithWorks offers a free, 13-week career development program, which includes developing the skills necessary for long-term employment; discovering strengths and taking responsibility for personal development and gainful employment; free individual and group counseling for students; participating in internships in local businesses of the students' choosing; weekly computer skills classes, as well as a Bible lesson; and developing friendships, skills, and maturity, which lead to sustained employment; and support for families and individuals. FaithWorks says "it's never too late to become what you might have been."

Five Talents

Vienna, Virginia
www.fivetalents.org

Five Talents fights poverty, creates jobs, and transforms lives by empowering the poor in developing countries through business training, microcredit programs, innovative savings, and spiritual development. Jobs are created through Five Talents' sound business training and micro-loans, which, together, quickly grow into small businesses. Some of its successful businesses involve food production and sales, street vending, brick manufacturing, shoe making, carpentry, auto repair, beauty salons, office services, and tailoring. These businesses service their immediate communities.

Five Talents works in partnership with other non-profits whose staff members have existing relationships in the communities, serving to expand and support the work of these non-profits. These partnerships also ensure good stewardship of resources in that Five Talents does not replicate the services of other organizations already serving in that community.

Good Soil, a ministry of Kingdom Causes

Bellflower, California
www.goodsoilindustries.com

Good Soil, a landscaping business, is "changing lives through work and mentorship." Good Soil takes referrals for potential employees who qualify as "hard to hire" and requires participation in classes before an individual becomes eligible for a part-time position. After proving themselves for at least two months in a part-time position, the employee then becomes eligible for a full-time position. Good Soil is a limited time program, with the goal of employees eventually obtaining permanent positions.

Homeboy Industries

Los Angeles, California
www.homeboy-industries.org

Homeboy Industries, with the motto "Nothing Stops a Bullet Like a Job," began in 1988 as Jobs for a Future, a program created by Father Greg Boyle. Father Boyle had been ministering in the parish of Boyle Heights for several years. His initiative grew out of his relationships with young men in gangs, as well as his concern to practically address the need for interventions. Homeboy Industries aims to assist at-risk and formerly gang-involved youth in becoming positive and contributing members of society through job placement. While "true change comes one day at a time, starting with a job," Homeboy Industries has grown to become a place of community, offering comprehensive services and specific job skills development, including solar panel installation and computer training. "Homeboy serves as a beacon of hope and opportunity for those seeking to leave gang life, for whom the barriers and challenges are great, and for whom there is virtually no other avenue to enter the mainstream." Starting with Homeboy Tortillas, Homeboy Industries' businesses have grown to include a bakery, diner, organic farm, cafe, catering, silk screening shop, and a clothing line.

After completing job readiness programs, clients are placed in one of the businesses to learn and apply work skills on the job, eventually becoming paid employees and earning a "living wage."

On Homebody Industries' blog, Rosa tells her story of how becoming pregnant motivated her to stop her involvement with gangs. During her pregnancy, she started looking for a job. "We'd leave at 7:00 in the morning and walk all day applying for jobs, with no money in our pockets. Finally I came to [Father Greg] . . . I just said 'I am pregnant, I need a job'. . . As soon as I got here, no one judged me . . . I learned responsibility, how to give up my attitude from the past, the vocabulary of being in a professional place." After working in Homeboy Industries for three years, Rosa was hired by another employer. For many of the employees, a desire to become better parents draws them to Homeboy Industries. Armando shares how, when his son was one month old, he was tempted to go back to drug dealing in order to provide for him. However, because of his belief that his son was an answer to his prayer, he instead went to Homeboy Industries to learn legitimate work. See Father Boyle's book, *Tattoos on the Heart*, for even greater perspectives.[14]

Jobs for Life

Raleigh, North Carolina
www.jobsforlife.org

Started in 1996 with a contractor looking for good employees and a pastor looking for employment opportunities for people in the church, Jobs for Life developed its motto: "Building lives, one job at a time." Jobs for Life seeks to "equip Christ-centered churches and organizations through the distribution of biblically based tools and materials to prepare individuals for work and life." The Jobs for Life "movement has developed a powerful, dependable, repeatable system, combining community immersion, neighbor-helping-neighbor, mentoring, instruction, learning, and coaching—all proceeding down a permanent path, and all rooted in the foundation of faith.

After one full year, usually between 70% and 80% of those who commit to follow the Jobs for Life way are still employed and living stable, growing lives. Currently, there are 236 organizations sponsoring Jobs for Life classes, mostly in mid-west and eastern areas of the United States. These organizations provide classes for adults and young people, with 16 sessions per class. Classes cover basic job program topics, as well as topics such as "my value as an employee," "understanding my life journey," and "taking responsibility for my actions." Organizations

---

[14] Gregory Boyle, *Tatoos on the Heart: The Power of Boundless Compassion*, Free Press, 2010.

that sponsor classes purchase a tool kit for $649, which includes a variety of instructor and student materials and support.

In Decatur, Alabama, the Neighborhood Christian Center sponsors Jobs for Life classes. Ashley, a woman leaving incarceration and attempting to find a job, was hesitant to take the classes. She assumed that she knew everything necessary to land a job: fill out an application, get called for an interview, and then get hired. However, after some encouragement, she decided to take the Jobs for Life classes at the Neighborhood Christian Center. Ashley says that she gained much more than job skills knowledge, but a personal understanding of who God created her to be, which gives her the confidence to live her life with a purpose.

Second Chance Coffee Company, LLC

Wheaton, Illinois
www.ihaveabean.com

Over weekly breakfast meetings, three friends began to dream and pray about how to use a business to "help transform the lives of former offenders." In 2007, Second Chance Coffee Company began with the premise of "using every part of [its] business to 'love our neighbors as ourselves' to positively impact the spiritual, social, and economic condition of our employees, their families, and the communities in which they live." The company roasts, packages, and delivers coffee and related products for its customers via online purchases. Recognizing that various challenges faced by former offenders are only partially met by employment, Second Chance Coffee collaborates with various faith-rooted organizations to further develop its employees.

JustWork Economic Initiative

Vancouver, British Columbia
www.justwork.ca

Growing out of the life of Grandview Calvary Baptist Church in Vancouver, British Colombia, JustWork provides job creation and training for people with significant barriers to employment—

physical disabilities, mental illnesses, homelessness, and addictions. The initiative offers safe places of employment, flexible hours and expectations, and relational commitment throughout the entire process. Separate programs exist in the areas of catering, construction renovation, pottery, and gardening. Participants gain marketable skills, as well as life skills and guidance through the commitment of Christian mentors and friendship. JustWork is a social enterprise in that it pursues both social and financial goals.

The King's Garden

Kasiglahan Village, Philippines
intervarsity.faithweb.com/kingsgarden/Home

The King's Garden is a for-profit farm, created by staff with a vision for developing a "farm within the city." On a rented plot of 3.5 hectares of land, farmers work together to grow organic produce to sell in local markets, with a profit to support families and sustain the farm. The King's Garden community creates "jobs, a healthy neighborhood, and a community that values work and the reward of the harvest," and functions as a context in which to live its values to steward God's creation, love God and neighbor, and make disciples. King's Garden dreams of growing beyond food production, with the intent of becoming a teaching farm and training center for youth.

Masterworks

Minneapolis, Minnesota
www.masterworksmpls.org

Masterworks was founded in 1991 by entrepreneur Tim Glader, who had a vision to hire those with significant barriers to employment. For the first 15 years, Masterworks derived 95% of its operating funds from its business profits. However, in 2006, Masterworks expanded its financial base in order to enhance the ministry focus "with a more intensive, holistic, individualized approach to the multi-layered needs of our participants" by creating a for-profit branch called Masterworks Manufacturing Systems, Inc., that helps fund the ministry and non-profit businesses.

The three non-profit businesses—which employ men full-time—include an auto maintenance business; a light assembly, manufacturing, and packaging business; and a construction remodeling business. Masterworks hopes for the construction business to expand into buying investment real estate to remodel and resell.

The non-profit businesses function as paid employment programs, with men graduating from the program in one to two years. Masterworks is "unashamedly Christian," spending time daily in prayer and Bible study with employees and talking about life issues in light of biblical truth as employees work alongside each other. Masterworks believes that "the greatest hope for lasting life changes is through a change in the heart."

Mission Ministries Philippines, Inc.'s Early Childhood Development Program

Manila, Philippines
www.mmpreschool.co.cc

This small, faith-rooted mission creates jobs for more than 1,500 impoverished women in 500 needy schools located in the slums of Manila. In 1984, Mission Ministries Philippines, Inc. (MMP) recognized the need for preschools that would prepare destitute children to enter the public school system, where it was not uncommon to have 100 first graders crowded into a single classroom and taught by one teacher. MMP believed that if a child knew how to read, write, and do basic math before entering a crowded classroom, he or she would have a good chance of succeeding in elementary school.

Starting small, the organization hired a teacher and trained her to teach social values, reading, writing, math, science, and social studies. Her initial success and the magnitude of the need encouraged MMP to expand. The organization found that it could provide training for teachers, and that it needed women who wanted to work and who had a love for children and a willingness to be used to bring children the "three R's" and God's values.

From the beginning, the organization decided it would not build a large school. Instead, it decided to invite churches to set up their own, respective schools, and MMP would help them operate these schools by training their teachers and administrators how to set up, manage, sustain, and expand their respective preschools. Impoverished, urban women trained for two years by MMP to become preschool teachers and administrators receive a stipend from the school through tuition fees and voluntary contributions. Churches own their schools, raise their own support, hire their own teachers, and elect a board that exists separately from the church. MMP is in partnership with these churches for two years. In that period, the schools receive discounts on the workbooks and other publications, and their teachers have the opportunity to sit in on seminars and be coached by supervisors. The strength of this approach lies in using the social movement paradigm of casting the vision of quality preschool education to partner churches, and investing in their capacity to initiate, own, sustain, and replicate their own preschools.

MMP staff members partnered with faculty members from the University of the Philippines Manila to develop a preschool curriculum. With a grant from a foundation, staff members authored workbooks, teacher manuals, and handbooks. MMP invests heavily on the job training of impoverished, urban women to become preschool teachers and administrators.

Youth Industry

San Francisco, California
www.youthindustry.org

Moved by compassion and faith for the large population of homeless youth in San Francisco, pediatrician Jake Sinclair and his wife Lee founded Youth Industry in 1993. They aim to assist homeless and at-risk youth in San Francisco and the Bay Area achieve self-sufficiency through a variety of vocational training and support services, such as mentoring and counseling. Knowing the challenges of employing homeless youth in typical jobs, they have chosen to do on-the-job training by creating small businesses to employ and develop youth. The first business was a bicycle repair shop, followed by thrift stores, a restaurant, a recycled merchandise operation, and a silk screening business. The youth not only gain job skills, but also confidence and self-esteem to move forward and off the streets. Youth Industry has provided full-time jobs for over 750 formerly homeless youth. In

2003, they began Youth Industry sister groups in Kenya to provide for homeless children and AIDS orphans in Kenya.

CONCLUSION

The diversity and creativity of each of these models clearly evidence the work of the Holy Spirit. God's people in each of these cities have tailored specific approaches appropriate for their respective city's context and needs in a way that utilizes the assets and resources available to God's people there. What we develop in our own city may end up borrowing concepts, components, or features from these examples, but will also reflect our own unique needs and assets.

As residents invested in the well being of Fresno, what can we learn from these noteworthy examples from other cities, tailoring wisdom from each to address our own challenges here? Can we try something together? Would your church or agency be open to investigating the possibilities, in partnership with others? Is anything too hard for God?

THREE

CASE STUDIES: Church- and Business-Based Models

By Randy White and Bryan Feil

CASE STUDY: Cornerstone Community Care Vocational Training Institute

Why does a church become involved in the creation of a vocational training school? In the case of Cornerstone Church in Downtown Fresno, it was because two things converged.

First, there was a need. Pastor Jim Franklin took seriously the needs he saw in his church and the wider community for job development. With chronic, double-digit unemployment and one of the highest rates of concentrated poverty of any large city in the United States, the need to develop employable skills in people paraded before him daily. Leading one of the larger and more ethnically and economically diverse congregations in Fresno, Pastor Franklin regularly saw the economic needs of people struggling to survive and clamoring for solutions that went beyond handouts and charity. Cornerstone had always been a compassionate congregation, reaching out to thousands who suffer from food insecurity, organizing food convoys to smaller communities blighted by agricultural calamity, initiating toy programs at Christmas for children caught in poverty, and more. Cornerstone was a symbol in the eyes of the local media of a compassionate congregation. Though grateful and willing to do these things, Pastor Franklin consistently discussed with his elders his hope of working toward longer-term, sustainable solutions. For him, that meant job training. He saw his role as "impregnating his people with vision, and then nurturing it along."[15]

---

[15] Personal interview with Pastor Jim Franklin, Dec. 14, 2011, Cornerstone Church, Fresno,

However, it was when this *need* converged with an *asset* that a solution was born. Having set a climate in his congregation compatible with this level of thinking, one of his elders came to him with a contact—someone they knew with a background in vocational training. This eventually led to the formation of the Cornerstone Vocational Training Institute, which formed into a separate 501(c)(3). The organization identified three areas of job training, partly as a result of available expertise in the church and partly for each area's potential for the immediate placement of graduates. These three areas were medical billing, auto repair, and culinary arts.

Of the three, medical billing proved to be the most successful, graduating—at its peak—20-25 participants at a time in successive classes with good placement rates. The auto repair facility required more of an upfront investment, including specialized equipment and a building rental. The Culinary Academy utilized Cornerstone Church's new conference center, which included a full commercial kitchen. Training approximately eight students at a time, participants in the Culinary Academy conducted on-the-job training, servicing the many community events, banquets, church, and civic meetings hosted at the conference center.

Funding for this creative effort came from three sources: the church itself, grants, and tuition paid by students. These three sources were sufficient to pay the salaries of the director and program coordinators. Cornerstone Church also maintained all facilities, so these overhead costs were not a factor. This funding formula worked well for a while, until the State of California altered the way student funding was distributed. Ultimately, reimbursements to the school came through students rather than directly from fund sources. Students didn't always complete the cycle to fully pay the school, thus creating problems. In addition, as the economy began to sour, grants began to dry up, not only to the Cornerstone Vocational Training Institute, but also to many vocational schools in general. Eventually, the situation was deemed unsustainable, and the institute closed.

The principles below can be extracted from the execution and eventual termination of this effort.

Lesson One: *Start with your assets.* A positive lesson learned is that churches wishing to move in this direction should use an approach to job training that utilizes the skill, knowledge, and expertise of people in your midst, as well as existing assets and resources. This may require utilizing a mechanism for taking an inventory of skills and knowledge in your church. Cornerstone Church had talented people in the area of culinary arts, auto repair, and medical billing, and, accordingly, was able to employ these skills in service of the program in a successful manner. In addition, the congregation had most of the facilities needed for each of these areas of focus. The exception was the shop for the auto repair, which required specialized space and equipment. In addition, a church-based approach has the ability to leverage caring volunteer help in the process of supporting those in training.

Lesson Two: *Do your homework, and then keep doing it.* Every asset needs supporting assets. Without these supporting assets, it may not be best to go down that road. Unfortunately, skills alone are not enough. Pastor Franklin feels that more market research would have been helpful to enable the church and its institute to prioritize their efforts into the most fruitful fields. The auto shop was costly to equip and never achieved sustainability. It was never able to engage more than four to five participants at a time and, due to the overhead, ended up not being cost-effective.

Lesson Three: *The Gospel and loving care must both take center stage.* Next, it is clear that it was the relational dimension that made each of these forms of training effective during the brief years of the program. Leaders shared not only their professional expertise with participants, but also their lives in the spirit of the Gospel. A church-based program can deal with the whole person and whole family, wrapping other forms of care and ministry around people's lives. This sets the program apart from other available forms of vocational training in the city. This is based on the knowledge that a holistic approach is needed when dealing with needs in people's lives—that employability is not only about acquiring employable skills, but about becoming a person of integrity, discipline, and consistency. Finally, from the Cornerstone Vocational Training Institute model, we learn that this form of job training needs structural improvements in two main areas to achieve its full potential. First, it must be taken to scale in order to do more than help a few individuals. With more than 40,000 unemployed or underemployed persons in our city, programs of this size cannot make a serious dent in the problem. Secondly, and perhaps related to the issue of scale, is the issue of sustainability. Programs like this tend to be the victims of the very kind of economic volatility they seek to address. For programs of this nature to be sustainable, as well as be taken to scale, several congregations would most likely need to partner together in a collaborative effort to share program costs, administration, facilities, leadership, and more. We might envision separate congregations throughout the city, each focusing on a different area of job training, linked together with other congregations doing a different area, utilizing a central administrative system and board.

Pastor Franklin and his team are to be commended for pioneering this effort, as well as thanked for the rich source of learning it provided for churches that will dare venture out in this direction.

CASE STUDY: Christian Temple

If starting a vocational training institute isn't for your congregation, Pastor Elias Loera of the Christian Temple has a model far less formal, but no less challenging. Pastor Eli is used to challenges. As a former United States Army Ranger, he routinely jumped out of airplanes, crashed through cement walls, and carried heavy weaponry in two wars. However, he knows the enemies he now faces—poverty and joblessness in Fresno—are powerful, and the war will not be won with force, but with creativity coupled with personal and congregational intentionality. This is the advocacy and mentoring model.

Before God called him to Fresno, he worked on the Washington State Migrant Council and for the Department of Labor's Job Placement service. He was well acquainted with the place and power of work in the lives of people to give them dignity, as well as the process to make it happen. Routinely finding work for those who had formerly only done farm labor turned out to be easier than anyone might have thought: once employers learned of the difficult conditions farm laborers endured before the crack of dawn during Washington winters, they eagerly hired them for many other positions. Yet, it was Eli's role as a pastor as a second job that taught him about a potential role the Church could play.

Working as a youth pastor for a second job, Eli found that five of his congregational members had trucking businesses and that they wanted drivers. So, to learn the certification process, he took the test himself. Once certified, he helped many others in need of work receive their own certifications. Near the end of his time as a youth pastor, he owned his own company and was running three big rigs himself.

The process of doing job placement for the government and the process of running his own company laid important foundations for his move to Fresno and his start as Pastor of the Christian Temple. He saw the power of advocacy in the Church, where human need often comes more visibly to the surface. It taught him that the Church can be a powerful tool for people who need work, if the following four key ingredients are in place.

First Ingredient: *A pastor must create a "culture of work" in the church.* Eli routinely "preaches employment," seeing the link between faith and work to be an issue of discipleship. If the subject is not important for the pastor, Eli believes that it won't be absorbed by the congregation. And he doesn't just preach employment; it surfaces in his counseling appointments, his youth mentoring, and his leadership meetings. Eli feels it necessary to orient the congregation in that direction, as well as oversee the overall application of this value and process, as Church leadership takes on the task of steering the unemployed toward opportunities. At the Christian Temple, there are three others in which he has invested who now have the necessary skills and knowledge in this area and who routinely walk people through the steps toward a job.

Second Ingredient: *A pastor must help members who are currently employed become advocates for members who are not.* Eli routinely helps members keep their eyes open for employment opportunities within their workplaces, and then to communicate openings through the congregation. He encourages them to commit to picking up new hires to ride together. He feels that there will never be enough programs in the city to cover all the need, but that churches who make this an intentional ministry of the church can bring a broader solution for the thousands of people invisible to traditional employment systems, but who are known to the church. This non-programmatic approach is crucial.

Regarding advocacy, Eli tells the story of Fran, a woman who came to his church because of a Vacation Bible School flyer. Fran was pretty rough herself and was accompanied by a man clearly in a gang. She had been on welfare for years, and had suffered through a series of abusive relationships. Through the church, her life began to stabilize. She was offered a job of cleaning houses by one of the women in the church. This position evolved into a job that combined cleaning and providing eldercare for five additional families. With a little margin in her life, she decided to go to Fresno City College to study business and, eventually, social work. She decided that she was indeed worth something, and decided to leave the man who had dragged her down with him. Through another contact in the church, she received a full-time job at a local elementary school. However, she has not forgotten how it all started: Fran now helps other women in her former situation to get cleaning jobs and even mentors them herself through that process.

Third Ingredient: *A pastor must integrate the issue of employment into the spiritual life of the congregation, as well as link it to individual and corporate spiritual journeys.* There should be prayer meetings designed specifically for those seeking employment or seeking to overcome significant barriers to employment. This is, in fact, happening all over the country—often called Job Clubs—sponsored by churches to provide support and care for people in need of work.

Fourth Ingredient: *A pastor must help his or her congregation as a whole grasp the desperation of those in our city who suffer from unemployment or underemployment.* A degree of insulation occurs when your own situation is secure and, in such a situation, it is too easy to lose touch with the human face of unemployment, as well as all of the surrounding painful circumstances. This can happen as urban and/or suburban church partnerships are created—as pastors form clusters in a geographic area and begin to share stories.

It's not jumping out of planes, and the primary weapon is different, but all hands are needed in this battle. Pastor Eli reminds us that with roughly 10,000 validated gang members; 6,000 homeless; and 43,000 unemployed in our city, we are up against a formidable challenge. Job-lessness is connected to every one of these subgroups. And even if every one of Fresno's 500 churches adopted a handful of individuals in these categories—which would be a genuine miracle—we still wouldn't be anywhere near close to winning this war. However, Pastor Eli reminds us that God's math is different, that the synergy created by churches in-tentionally applying the above ingredients often changes the equation, and what God can accomplish doesn't always make sense "on paper." The first question for us all will be this: *Are we in God's army together?*

CASE STUDY: J&D Foodservice

A local Fresno County business, J&D Foodservice has given many op-portunities to local agencies such as Hope Now for Youth, The Fresno Rescue Mission's Academy program, and Workforce Connection. Mark Ford, one of the partners of J&D and Certified Meat Products, sees the business as having a vital role in the Kingdom of God. With all the ex-periences that Mark has gleaned in providing individuals with barriers to employment a chance, he sees that every individual has a major deci-sion that needs to be made. They need to want to work, instead of just have a need for a job. There are a lot of individuals who need work, but significantly less are *willing* to work and *eager* to jump at any available employment opportunity.

This is the biggest obstacle for J&D when it offers employment op-portunities to entry-level employees. Mark challenges local agencies working to combat unemployment to specifically target individuals who really want to work. Until an individual reaches that point, placing him or her in a job will be a challenge. Within job training programs, Mark has also seen that these individuals need to understand the impor-tance of common workplace practices: good communication, providing a two weeks notice when other opportunities arise, how reputations are important within the job market, and more.

J&D has had many successful placements through job development or-ganizations, as well. "Hector," who currently works at J&D, was hired through Hope Now For Youth and has been an employee for six years. One of the most liked and driven employees, he is on his way to becom-ing a shift supervisor and has been a great asset to J&D.

J&D is effective because—motivated by faith—the business seeks those employees who, regardless of where they have been, are prepared with a positive attitude and willingness to work. In addition, the business also maintains a flexible, patient, and committed posture toward those they hire, setting high standards while simultaneously recognizing the reality that people who have been on the margins of the work world often need to gradually grow into a new way of living, acquiring the skills and disciplines to serve them well over the long haul.

CASE STUDY: Cal Custom Tile

The story of Cal Custom Tile, a company owned and operated in Fresno for the past 31 years, is one of grace and success from both worldly and Kingdom perspectives. Rick Berry, who started the company, has employed thousands within Fresno County.

Like many construction companies, a significant percentage of employees have dealt or are currently dealing with drug or alcohol abuse and/or gang involvement. Rick has learned to deal with employees differently based on their attitudes and resources, as well as their openness to receive help for their problems. Unfortunately, however, some employees have been released in situations of theft. From an employer's perspective, however, Rick has learned that if true life-change is going to happen and new creations are going to be formed, we—employers, family members, and co-workers—have to be willing to be there for them, especially when things get messy. Yet, there does come a time when individuals eventually see what the outcome of their decisions will be if they continue on the paths of abuse and addiction. For agencies working on training potential employees, Rick lists the following as what he values most in potential workers:

1. Promptness and being prepared for work

2. Knowing how to deliver good customer service

3. Being able to follow through on the job site

4. Eager to learn and able to follow instructions, as well as willing to listen to those with experience

5. An ability to have the quality of their work evaluated

6. Reliable and consistent transportation

Rick counsels other business owners who want to give a second chance to workers with barriers to employment to regard this endeavor as a ministry and to depend on the Holy Spirit. Although working with challenging individuals often poses problems, Rick views it as a calling. He also reminds us that sometimes it works, and sometimes it doesn't. When it doesn't, he suggests that we have to commit the worker to the grace of God and move them on. However, seeing individuals who have succeeded and come out on the other side has been a real highlight, as well as the core of what makes Cal Custom Tile what it is today.

FOUR

We Can Do It & We Are Doing It:
Local Examples of Faith-Rooted Agencies Doing
Job Creation, Job Training, or Job Placement

By Artie Padilla

Historically, Fresno's economic base has been an agricultural one. The city sits right in the middle of our planet's most fertile geographic region and, as such, functions as the fruit basket of the world. This is a wonderful gift to both the local and global economies, but the context creates a challenge. As our city has grown in population, we have not been able to diversify our economy. Although we do have some large manufacturing and retail businesses in Fresno, the employment opportunities they present are simply not sufficient to deal with the scale of Fresno's employment challenges. For so many, living here is like living in the "empty tip of the Horn of Plenty."[16]

When combining this fact with other realities such as a large immigrant population (language and cultural challenges), high dropout rates (lack of educational attainment), and growing concentrated poverty (numerous neighborhoods where the poverty rate exceeds 40%), we get a community whose access to sustainable financial stability has been out of reach for generations.

However, a light has been dawning over the last two decades. On a civic level, there have been recent changes that help promote Fresno as an attractive area for job development. Our mayor has launched a series of food expos designed to feature and promote our most abundant resource:

---

[16] Randy White used this phrase at an international conference in Holland in 2001.

our ability to grow just about anything and develop it into desirable products. These expos themselves have helped launch new businesses.

Looking intentionally at our assets and resources—especially in the faith community of our city—we see hope. God has raised up many of our city's churches and faith-rooted Community Benefit Organizations (CBOs) to specifically address core issues related to employment in our community.

In our research, we saw many local CBOs—though limited in capacity due to funding—with a deep passion and unique skills to empower and walk alongside individuals previously unemployed, underemployed, or with significant barriers to employment.

We will share a few stories from some of them, as well as offer some data on their strengths or limitations. At the end of the chapter, you will find a directory of ministries currently working to build relationships and skills in order to help people become economically self-sustaining. We have also included some local and effective non-faith-rooted agencies in an appendix; we have an enormous task before us and, as such, varied approaches are welcome.

WHAT WE'VE LEARNED FROM OUR OWN BACKYARD

1. Think Thrift

During the current recession, thrift stores have outpaced retail stores in sales percentage increases. Because of this, it shouldn't be a surprise to see thrift stores becoming integrated into the ministry strategies of Fresno's faith community. However, did you know this is a job training strategy? Although we have several in this city, I'll share a bit about two thriving models.

Highway City Thrift Store has been in existence since 1983. Its vision is to provide economic development in an under-resourced section of Fresno. Highway City does this by providing some job training at the store: customers can also earn groceries and clothes with volunteer service for the store. This concept provides customers with a sense of dignity in knowing they earned their product rather than it simply being given to them as charity.

Highway City also has a community service program with the court system that allows non-violent offenders to serve at the store to earn their community service requirements. This not only provides them a place to serve their hours, but an environment showered in God's grace and love where genuine relationships can be built.

The store is located in a part of Fresno called Highway City—a small area incorporated into Fresno in 1983 around Shaw and Highway 99. This area has been chronically under-resourced, and its isolation is now exacerbated by it being "cocooned" by new housing developments. Gang activity, poverty, drugs, and a general lack of readily accessible services have led to the development of Highway City Community Development.

The second example is *Neighborhood Thrift*. Much like Highway City Thrift Store, Neighborhood Thrift was birthed as a ministry from a local church. The Well Community Church began an outreach in central Fresno in 2002 and, as the church and outreach began to grow, the congregation started to give unwanted clothes, furniture, and other household goods to their ministry team. These were then given to the families in their neighborhood with whom they had build relationships. By 2005, people were donating so many goods that the church's storage sheds were constantly full and the team couldn't donate them quickly enough. At the same time, a graduate of the Pink House Center for Urban Ministry Training, run by the Fresno Institute for Urban Leadership wanted to mix his business degree with his desire for ministry. God was in the mix, and the thrift store took shape.

Its first year, 2008, was spent in a 2,000-square-foot location in Fresno's Tower District. Neighborhood Thrift quickly outgrew that building and, a year later, it proceeded to move into a 20,000-square-foot location about a mile away. Neighborhood Thrift's vision for the new store included a "community area," where activities and events took place to benefit the surrounding neighborhood residents. Some of these events include community meetings, financial education workshops, resume and job application skills workshops, community concerts, and a safe-place drop in center for youth in the afternoons. An example of the flow of Neighborhood Thrift's ministry from early on was its introduction to

Sandra, the store's back warehouse supervisor. Sandra's kids were engaged in The Well's Saturday morning youth program at their school in 2002. Through its connection with her kids, The Well slowly built a relationship with Sandra. At that time, she was struggling financially and not able to find a self-sustaining job in an enjoyable environment. When The Well first opened up Neighborhood Thrift, Sandra was quick to volunteer. Though there were no promises that she would get a job, she consistently showed up to help. Once the store moved to the larger location in 2009 and sales began to increase, Sandra was one of its first hires.

It didn't take her long to become a supervisor and she is now growing in knowledge and confidence with each passing month. It will be her 10-year anniversary coming up this year, a relationship that started with The Well loving her kids to helping her better provide for her family. This is what Sandra had to say when asked of her experience at Neighborhood Thrift:

> This has been a great dream and blessing to be part of a family-like working environment. Compared to my past jobs, Neighborhood Thrift has allowed me to grow as a person and an employee. The experiences that I have gained and the responsibilities that are given me are very new, but also very appreciated. I feel like a woman of worth! This has also allowed me to have a more stabile life for my family at home. The kids can see me every night and I can spend more time with them.

There are other churches that have started smaller size thrift stores within Fresno, as well. All of these stores have a vision to build relationships, as well as to financially support some of their other ministries.

2. From Gangs to Jobs

Fresno's young adults have many paths down which to walk. Unfortunately, many of those paths are unhealthy and spiritually dead. Our city is riddled with clusters of gangs in our neighborhoods, and many of our youth and young adults connect more with them than with our educational institutions and faith communities.

However, *Hope Now for Youth* is an extremely successful ministry that provides young men involved in gangs with an off-ramp from that life and on-ramp into an environment that allows them to grow spiritually with the Lord while equipping them in the area of job readiness.

From 1993 to 2010, Hope Now For Youth had placed 1,700 men between the ages of 16 and 24 in jobs with nearly 300 businesses in Fresno. Within that, they've had an 85% success rate with those placed. Most of these youth were on parole or probation and around 65% of them were high school dropouts. In 2012, a feature-length film has been released based on this story.

On a different tier of engagement, Laneesha Senegal with *Helping Others Pursue Excellence (HOPE)* has implemented a unique strategy to teach young men simple trades. She hopes that they will embrace one trade in particular and that it moves them in a direction of going to vocational school. At one of west Fresno's community centers, she has set up a program where these men can gain skills in carpentry, plumbing, and electrical. For those with an entrepreneurial mind, she provides guidance and training for them to someday start a small business. Here's what one of the youth involved in HOPE said about his experience:

> This is the first time someone has shown an interest in what I can become as a person. No one, even in my family, thought I would amount to much. Learning the trade of plumbing has given me the confidence to get a real job so I can take care of my little boy. The world looks so much different when you have a positive experience like this. Being able to take care of me and my family makes me feel good about myself.

3. Fresno's Amazing Pot of Stew

An incredibly diverse place, Fresno boasts more than 85 languages, as well as a host of clearly defined subcultures. Because of this, educating and equipping people to join our local workforce is nothing short of a unique challenge. In our experience, we came across the following groups, which we want to highlight for their effectiveness in dealing with these challenges.*Fresno Interdenominational Refugee Ministries (FIRM)* has a culturally sensitive and relational employment program for our city's refugees. This program includes employment appraisals, case management, and job placement. FIRM has enjoyed great success in serving our Southeast Asian, Slavic, and African refugees over the last 16 years and we are now seeing many of these former new Americans becoming community leaders and advocating for the upcoming generation of newcomers. FIRM has become a huge asset to our city, residents, and local churches.

The *Fresno Rescue Mission (FRM)* is a strong ministry anchor in our city. Started in 1949, its vision is to those in a season of life without hope or purpose. In the area of job readiness, the FRM currently has a program to equip men with skills in areas such as landscaping, janitorial services, and auto mechanic work. The FRM also have GED, literacy, and other tutoring programs to help those in need throughout their process of job preparedness. The FRM program is much too extensive to explain here, but you can learn more by going to its website. An extension of the Fresno Rescue Mission is *Samaritan Women*, a focused ministry that empowers abused and/or addicted women to return to being healthy, productive women of God. An aspect of this transformation is becoming someone with the life skills, disciplines, and abilities that an employer desires. Samaritan Women offers job skills, computer training, and general office and telephone skills. Samaritan Women is currently renovating a former motel in west-central Fresno, where it can expand its services to teach participants food preparation and restaurant-related skills.

Two other notable ministries that focus on empowering women are the *Evangel Home* and *My Sister's Closet*. Job readiness is a required part of the program at Evangel Home while the women stay on its campus. The Evangel Home sees this as part of its holistic approach of building up an entire person. My Sister's Closet also focuses on a woman's work and career development with conferences throughout the year for women to learn, engage, and network. These conferences are followed up with the women receiving professional attire for their upcoming job interviews.

4. Common Themes

As we examined all of these models, as well as the ones featured at the end of this chapter, the following five common themes, elements, or key principles rose to the surface:

1. *Relationships*: Each group saw the value of building a trusting relationship with the people they served. This took time and intentionality, but was integral to the health and success of each.
2. *Follow-Up*: This went hand-in-hand with relationships. Follow-up was vital in the building of trust, as well as the continuation of guidance in creating paths to job readiness and financial security.
3. *Multi-Faceted Outreach*: With relationship-building as the basis, these efforts all built upon that foundation by intentionally addressing other key issues, such as financial education, family health, and spiritual health.
4. *Sector-Specific*: Nearly all of these models served people receiving some form of government assistance, living on unemployment for an extended amount of time, or having never been employed in the past.
5. *Collaborative Visions*: For the sake of sharing resources, many were working with other non-profits to help bring in other services to the individuals they served.

SUMMARY & CHALLENGE: HOW DO WE EAT AN ELEPHANT?

These are but a few spotlights on ministries that actively address one aspect or another of job creation, training, or placement in our city. Some may feel it is overwhelming to think of what it would take to do what these agencies do. However, it must be emphasized that each of these great outreaches started as small efforts, by either a church or a small group of individuals being called by the Lord to serve families here in Fresno who were on the margins, in part by their difficulties in being employable.

What would it take for us to fan the flames of these models into a wildfire? What would it take to mobilize the talents and resources of the some 500 churches and 100 Christian non-profits in the city to build economic stability to the families with whom we share a destiny? What would it take to utilize the resources of your church to start something small? If you pastor a church, how might your congregation be enlisted to address the task of helping our residents become economically self-sufficient? What if Fresno's more than 500 churches all did something small in the areas of job creation, readiness training, or placement? What would happen? At the very least, we can all commit to supporting those attempting it, especially those on the following list.

How do we eat an elephant? Not one bite at a time. Instead, we invite everyone to the table for a thousand small bites.

LOCAL EXAMPLES

ARC Fresno

Lori Ramirez, *Executive Director*
4567 N. Marty Ave.
Fresno, CA 93722
(559) 226-6268
loriramirez@arcfresno.org
Target Population: Developmentally disabled

ARC Fresno is an important provider of services that educate and enrich the lives of individuals with developmental disabilities. It offers everyday life experiences in a supportive community. Some of the educational classes offered include cooking, computers, community college courses, and music.

Fresno Bridge Academy

May Ly, *Case Manager*
Reading And Beyond Admin. Office
4819 E. Butler Ave.
Fresno, CA 93727
(559) 454-8810
mly@readingandbeyond.org

Target Population: Unemployed and under-employed

Fresno Bridge Academy, a job readiness program, is designed to help eligible unemployed and under-employed adults become employed or job-ready. Its goal is to help 120 participants achieve and maintain self-reliance by completing a job readiness program. A full-time case manager ensures each participant's success, creating a unique approach that sees the individual through a holistic lens.

Evangel Home

Gerre Brenneman, *Executive Director*
137 N. Yosemite Ave.
Fresno, CA 93701
(559) 2640-4717
director@evangelhome.org
Target Population: Homeless women

A job readiness course is a mandatory part of the program curriculum for GARDEN and Crossroads program residents. Additionally, graduates of these two Evangel Home programs who choose to remain with Evangel Home as a resident in the Community Connections program will receive further assistance in job readiness, as well as guidance in employment opportunities.

Feed My Sheep Ministries

Fresno Inner-City Job Placement Center
Pastor Bruce Hood
(559) 978-5469
Target Population: Unemployed and under-employed

This ministry assists Fresno businesses, at no cost, with preparing applicants for job readiness. Training programs for participants cover application prep, interviewing skills, resume writing, identification prep, and appropriate attire, as well as follow-up and mentoring.

Fresno Interdenominational Refugee Ministries (FIRM)

Paula Cha, *Employment Program Director*

1940 N. Fresno Street
Fresno, CA **93703**
(559) 487-1500
Target Population: Refugees

The FIRM Employment Program focuses on providing culturally sensitive employment services to the refugee population of Fresno County. Clients may obtain services Monday through Friday, from 8:30 a.m. to 5:00 p.m., though appointments are preferred.

Services FIRM provides include, but are not limited to the following: assessment, case management, referral to community services, resume, interview skills, job applications, job search/assisted/unassisted/online, labor market information, job behavior, on-the-job training, job development and placement services, follow-up on the job, ESL, VESL, and other related employment activities.

Fresno Rescue Mission (FRM)

The Academy Rehabilitation Program For Men
Bud Searcy, *Academy Director*
310 G St.
Fresno, CA 93706
(559) 268-0839, ext. 115
bsearcy@fresnorescuemission.org

Javier Garza, *Academy Coordinator/Employment Specialist*
(559) 268-0839, ext. 127
jgarza@fresnorescuemission.org
Target Population: Men

The Academy is an 18-month Christian life-change program for men, featuring one year of in-patient and six months of out-patient. This is a work-based program, during which outside jobs are prohibited. During the one-year in-patient program, men are assigned to work squads and have the opportunity to receive job skills training in the following areas: landscaping, culinary, security, customer service, janitorial, maintenance, administrative office, warehousing, auto mechanics, car detailing, and auto sales. As part of their work therapy, the men receive monthly work evaluations in order to identify work-rated behaviors, ethics, and attitudes that need correcting. A job specialist meets with them to coach them on overcoming these areas. The Academy also has Life Skills classes throughout the in-patient program that include handling finances, developing communication skills, handling our emotions, stress management, and problem solving skills. Furthermore, GED, literacy classes, and individual tutors are offered. The program pays for GED tests.

In the last ten weeks of the in-patient program, men in their fourth quarter of the program go through a ten-week job readiness workshop. This includes resume development, interview skills, tips for job search and interviews for ex-offenders and felons, determining your career path, mock interviews, and more. Participants are also able to search for a job. The FRM is continuously expanding its employer network. The program also provides tailored suits and dress clothes suitable for interviews. Additionally, a class helps develop the soft skills necessary to succeed on the job once employed. Topics in this class include employer expectations, good work ethics, communication skills on the job, solving job related problems and conflicts, and more. Pre-employment background checks and financial assistance towards forklift certifications are provided. Finally, a fund is established to help the men obtain a valid California ID or driver's license and a social security card.

Super Thrift Store and Cars
181 East Sierra
Fresno, CA 93710
(559) 440-0868

The thrift store is used as a vocational training center, providing job training for men and women in the FRM's recovery programs.

Highway City Community Development (HCCD)

Jeff Harrington
4710 N. Polk
Fresno, CA 93722
(559) 271-8869
jeffrycraig.harrington@gmail.com

Highway City Thrift Store
Sue Sloper
5472 W. Shaw
Fresno, CA 93722
(559) 275-6677
Target Population: Underserved

The purpose of Highway City Community Development is to transform Highway City and the Central Unified School communities by stimulating the economic, physical, and spiritual infrastructures of those communities through indigenous leadership. One of its values is that education and vocational training are key components of community strength.

HCCD has a work program where an individual can earn two bags of non-perishable groceries for two hours of work through its store. Two more hours of work will buy $17 worth of clothing, and four hours buys $27 worth of clothing. Individuals can also work for furniture. The amount of time worked depends on the value of the items. Additionally, a community service program exists for non-violent offenders to perform court-ordered community service hours.Participants in the program work in Highway City and its surrounding communities to stimulate economic development and enlist indigenous leadership to improve the economic, physical, and spiritual infrastructures, thereby bringing hope and stabilization to families in the community. This is accomplished through vocational training; a dignity-based philosophy where people can work for food, clothing, appliances, and furniture; a ten-month incarnational internship for training future leaders for urban ministry; afterschool programs; and summer enrichment programs. This is accomplished through partnerships with over a dozen other agencies.

Hogar Ministries

Ernesto Escalante, *Founder/CEO*
2014 Tulare Street, Suite 635
Fresno, CA 93721
(559) 472-7340
Target Population: Low-income, underserved, underprivileged, mentally challenged individuals

Hogar Ministries is a family and community outreach program. Opportunities for service include finding one's purpose in life, positive thinking skills, life skills mentoring, marketable skills assessment, career analysis and development, vocational training referrals, interviewing techniques, resumes, job search, placement and retention.

Hope Now For Youth

Roger Feenstra, *Executive Director*
2305 Stanislaus St.
Fresno, CA 93721
(559) 237-7215
info@hopenow.org
Target Population: 16-24 year-old men

Hope Now For Youth employs former Hope Now youth whose lives have changed to serve as both role models and vocational placement counselors who find gainful employment for at-risk young men, ages 16 to 24. As of January 1, 2011, Hope Now For Youth had placed nearly 1,700 youth—most of whom are gang members with criminal records—in jobs with 300 Fresno area businesses with an 85% success rate and an 8% recidivism rate. Almost all of these youths are on parole or probation, and over 65% are school dropouts. Hope Now For Youth's services are free of charge for both the businesses involved and the participating men.

Love and Garlic

Nancy Bajretti, *Founder and Head Chef*
90 E. Escalon, Suite 127
Fresno, CA 93710
nvgarlic@att.net
(559) 438-8677

Nancy's purpose is to help train people in the catering and banquet industry in Fresno. This takes place over the course of a few weeks. She personally helps place them in jobs.

Nancy's vision is to assist those interested in food service to gain understanding and experience by training at her business. She understands the importance of building up a person emotionally, spiritually, physically, and with work skills. As the person gleans experience, Nancy provides references and referrals as he or she applies for other jobs.

Mary Ella Brown (MEB) Community Center

Rena Jaso
(559) 266-0600
Target Population: Adults and High School Students

The MEB Community Center has become a local hub of informational resources for the southwest Fresno community. The center offers soft skills training for adults, as well as simple resume and application workshops at the computer lab on-site. MEB is part of a neighborhood collaboration focusing on revitalization and job readiness.

My Sister's Closet, a ministry of United Faith Fellowship

Yami Rodriguez
4410 E. Grant
Fresno, CA 93702
(559) 458-0229
yamiredriguez@yahoo.com
Target Population: Underserved women

My Sister's Closet empowers and equips underserved women on their journey to self-sufficiency through a holistic approach in career development and provision of nearly new professional attire. This program consists of two career development conferences each year for the women to learn interviewing and resume building skills. Following the conference, the participating women receive professional clothing and model their clothing at a Runway Show graduation.

Neighborhood Thrift

Bryan Feil, *Store Director*
353 E Olive Avenue
Fresno, CA 93728
(559) 498-0708

info@neighborhoodthrift.com
Target Population: Employees, welfare to work participants and others in need of work experience.

Economic development and job creation are essential to Neighborhood Thrift's vision. In addition to providing hands-on work experience as a stepping stone to becoming successful in the job market, NT envisions future efforts in small business development.

Northpointe Church

Northpointe Works Ministry
Carlotta Curti
4625 W. Palo Alto Ave.
Fresno, CA 93722
(559) 276-2300
Carlotta.c@comcast.net
Target Population: Unemployed

This ministry of Northpointe Church was designed for people who are unemployed and having difficulty getting back into the job market. The primary design of this ministry is to facilitate networking between unemployed individuals and business leaders, as well as to provide encouragement during this stressful time.

Poverello House

Daytime Shelter
412 F Street
Fresno, CA 93706
(559) 442-4108
Target Population: Homeless families

The Poverello House provides individual, need-based support to the people it serves. Some of these services include application assistance, resume writing help, and appointment making.

The Salvation Army

Dwaine Breazeale

1914 Fulton Street
Fresno, CA 93721
(559) 233-0139
Dwaine.Breazeale@usw.salvationarmy.com
Target Population: Prisoner rehabilitation

Through cooperative arrangements with prison, probation, and parole officials throughout the country, The Salvation Army plays a growing role in prison rehabilitation and crime prevention. In some jurisdictions, prisoners are paroled to the direct custody of The Salvation Army. Local services offered include Bible correspondence courses, prerelease job-training programs, employment opportunities in cooperation with parole personnel, material aid, and spiritual guidance to both prisoners and their families.

Samaritan Women

Deborah Torres, *Program Director*
4840 N. First Street, Suite 110
Fresno CA 93726
(559) 227-2190
dtorres@fresnorescuemission.org
Target Population: Women released from prison

Samaritan Women offers job skills, including training in computers (certificates of completion are available for typing, Microsoft Word, Microsoft Excel, and Microsoft PowerPoint), as well as general office and telephone skills. Additionally, Samaritan Women has deployed career employment services specifically for women in rehabilitation, helping them overcome barriers such as criminal history, lack of education, lack of stability, and more. An employment specialist works closely with the men in small groups and one-on-one. Candidates are required to come to class "dressed for success" in proper professional work attire, and mock interviews are conducted and reviewed by classmates. Computers are available for online job searches and, once an interview is arranged, women are trained to handle the interview process in a positive manner.

St. Joseph's Community Center and Thrift Shop

Leon Santos
(559) 363-3277
Target Population: Store employees

Leon Santos started this ministry with the vision of providing training in the area of retail through employment at the thrift store. His vision also included training in the areas of construction and agriculture. Some of the ways the store assists individuals is in getting them trained in working the register, surveying inventory, and stocking items. These individuals are also provided clothes for their first interviews. In addition, the community center serves as a place for individuals to be equipped and mentored throughout the job-training process.

FIVE

Possible Next Steps for Your Church or Agency

By Jeff Harrington and Bud Searcy

NEXT STEPS *(Jeff Harrington)*

For several years, I have reflected on the concept that God actually created work for the one portion of His creation made in His image. He did this before sin broke into humankind's history. Through work, God gave all of us a tangible, daily means by which to bring Him honor and glory, as well as marvel at His power.

The ramifications of understanding this element of God's creative process should radically realign our sense of our responsibilities in our respective ministry outlets. Work is a vital part of the human existence. Dorothy Sayer wrote, ". . . work is not, primarily, a thing one does to live, but the thing one lives to do."[17] As such, unemployment is not simply a psychological or emotional trauma or simply a financial hardship on the individual, family, or society. Instead, unemployment is a deeply spiritual trauma because work is part of God's design for how we can purposely worship Him each and every day of our lives. This makes the issues of work, employment placement, training, and financial education highly missional in nature.

As the appointed vessel of transformation, the Church should seek ways to minister to the vocational needs of the people. The following sections will not only address possible options for the Church

---

[17] Gilbert C. Meliander, ed., *Working: Its Meaning and its Limits* (Notre Dame, IN: University of Notre Dame Press, 2000), 43.

to pursue, but also vehicles by which people can be taught to better steward the income produced by their employment.

BUSINESS ADVISOR *(Jeff Harrington)*

Informal—also known as illegal—income has always been part of a society's production capacity. Most would understand this to be on the more nefarious side of the black market, which includes the sale and distribution of illicit drugs and the facilitation of prostitution.

However, there is another side of this type of informal income which is "legitimate" in nature, yet societal hurdles, bureaucratic "red tape," and a general distrust of governmental policies create an environment in which genuine, needed products are produced and sold informally. Unfortunately, this robs the tax increment upon which many civic services such as roads, sewers, police and fire departments, and more depend.

In Diego Winkelrid's abstract "Income distribution and the size of the informal sector,"[18] he sites that the informal income of the country of Mexico is roughly 30% of its GNP. This fact contributes significantly to ongoing struggles in the general population of the country. Fresno is ripe for this type of economy to form, due to the substantial lack of employment opportunities. How can this be addressed?

Picture a coalition of churches coming together and providing a significant missional opportunity to the members of congregations who have started businesses and/or are in significant management positions. These *business advisors* would step in and help business owners running informal—illegal, non-permitted—businesses to become legal business entities. These contacts would be made through churches, which could invest resources through the advisors to train the business operators in the benefits of becoming a legal business, management and leadership, proper bookkeeping and accounting, biblically based ethics and legal help, and navigating the permitting process.

This issue of teaching biblically based ethics is significant in the overall transformational work of the Church. A coalition of churches needs to

---

[18] Diego Winkelrid, Income distribution and the size of the informal sector, , October 25, 2005, pg 16
http://www.rrojasdatabank.info/inequality/SSRN-id777144.pdf (accessed January 4, 2012)

insure that the business advisors being raised up—raised up as "missionaries"—are teaching biblical ethics that support the idea that pursuing jobs for the sake of jobs alone is an empty, shallow, and even detrimental pursuit. Churches must promote that we "cannot rely on a simplistic formula that allows economic activity to be free-wheeling and relies on government and political structures alone to assure that the wealth created is equitably distributed."[19] Wealth creation goes terribly astray without biblical ethics being practiced. As Pope Benedict XVI has written, "The economy needs ethics in order to function correctly—not any ethic whatsoever, but an ethic which is people-centered."[20]

SOCIAL INVESTING GROUPS *(Jeff Harrington)*

Many American churches understand and even contribute through their mission budgets toward micro lending in developing countries. Donating $35 to West African Vocational Schools (WAVS) could help a woman start a business as a seamstress. A small donation of $5 through Wycliffe will help a family in Papua New Guinea purchase two baby chickens to develop the ability to sell eggs and raise more chickens to sell.

Micro lending in the United States looks very different—although the same in principal—due to the size and nature of our economy. In short, in the United States, it takes considerably more capital to start a business and to train an individual to run that business properly. This is where Social Investing Groups (SIG) come into the picture.

SIGs are formal funding groups, which invest in a variety of important social concerns in a community. Many of these groups look toward addressing environmental factors and affordable housing. Some SIGs might have a vision and mission to help assess a Community Benefit Organization's (CBO) ability to generate a positive, effective, and measurable outcome to its work. Should these organizations show the ability to be high-performing and generate social value to their community, funds would then be invested to strengthen the capacity and sustainability of that CBO's work.

---

[19] Larry Snyder, *Think and Act Anew: How Poverty in America Affects Us All and What We Can Do About It*, (Maryknoll, New York: Orbis Books, 2010), 63.

[20] Ibid, 63.

As with any investment group, the organizations assess the ability of their investments to bring about a financial return. However, the key factor is that return on investment can be reasonably assumed and the under-resourced community can gain traction toward over-all health. This tends to be the stated vision and mission of these organizations. For instance, the Trident Social Investment Group's vision statement is "The Trident Social Investment Group will be a 'Beacon of Hope' to disadvantaged communities in the 'Age of Austerity' and beyond."[21]

Perhaps your church could gather people of means and start a SIG. I encourage you to start small, investigate what others have done, and see what develops.

INDIVIDUAL DEVELOPMENT ACCOUNT *(Jeff Harrington)*

As important as employment and job training are, it would be unwise for agencies to neglect the importance of training people in financial proficiency. Beneficial toward this goal, Individual Development Accounts (IDAs) are savings accounts in which the individual deposits funds, which are then matched at varying degrees. The accounts are targeted to meeting specific financial goals. Depending on the program or institution, they may used toward home buying, education, or even starting or building the capacity of an existing business run by the person trained.

IDAs were developed from a philosophy that "traditional poverty pro-grams that focus on income transfers such as Temporary Assistance for Needy Families payments or food stamp benefits, are necessary, but meet only short-term consumption needs."[22] This process helps teach the individual the importance of building assets in order to build a fi-nancial reserve to address emergencies and build toward future goals. Asset-based proponents contend that this type of accumulation of as-sets "over a longer time horizon creates a financial cushion for emer-gencies, which in turn generates social, behavioral, and psychological benefits. Armed with assets, an individual's options for emerging from

---

[21] http://www.trident-ha.org.uk/about-us/our-vision-mission-and-values/ (accessed January 4, 2012)

[22] FDIC Quarterly, 2007, volume 1, No. 1, 22

poverty and entering the financial mainstream are greatly enhanced."[23]

IDAs are often formed through CBOs, as well as financial institutions. A significant element to establishing this type of asset-base ministry is the requirement that individuals participate in a financial proficiency course. Wouldn't that be a simple and helpful piece for churches to contribute? Churches could either start their own, or assist an organization in running one.

ANNUAL PRIMERS FOR CHURCH LEADERS *(Jeff Harrington)*

It is not an overstatement to say that most pastoral leaders have a small amount of business acumen, as this simply was not a significant part of their training for pastoral ministry. Their primary role has been to provide spiritual direction through the preaching of the Word, praying, and providing spiritual guidance, and this takes most of their time. Pastors and Christian non-profit leaders often have not had time to learn basic business practices, or even what services exist in a city to help someone run their own business. However, pastoral leaders usually have any number of capable business people within their congregations. These leaders can be gathered annually, and presented with practical information directed at educating them on the community's employment climate, needs, and coming trends.

But, what if we also invited civic leaders who could equip pastors to understand how to access and use city resources? Most pastors face, every day, unemployed or under-employed people in their congregations. Many pastors aren't sure how to respond, or even what resources exist in a city to help members of their congregations in this predicament. What if there was an annual meeting designed by elected officials and leaders in the civic, non-profit community to educate pastors about the options and resources at their disposal?

Abundant Communities is a movement started by Peter Block and John McKnight that counters the materialism and consumerism creating such dysfunction in our society today. They believe that the gifts, talents, abilities, and even passions needed to transform a community already exist in the various segments of that community. Block and McKnight

---

[23] Ibid, 22.

endorse the gathering of leaders in the fields of education, government, business, health, and religion to begin networking and understanding what each sector can offer.

ACCESSIBLE CONGREGATIONAL STEPS *(Jeff Harrington)*

One of the most concrete and ministry-oriented activities a church body can supply for those stuck in unemployment is the formation of a "job club." A job club functions in "helping unemployed community members find a new job and manage the challenges associated with unemployment."[24] Job clubs do not just work with the unemployed to help with resumes, leads, or training, but they also serve to help the emotional and psychological issues associated with job loss.

Ben Van Arragon states, "What often stands in the way for people in the job search isn't their qualifications. It's the way they feel about themselves and their job loss . . . In talking through the underlying emotions of job loss, people are able to let go of some of the negative feelings as they approach interviews and write résumés."[25]

Church leaders who have developed this type of ministry are seeing genuine transformation take place not only among church members, but also in reaching individuals outside the confines of the Church. Elissa Cooper of Menlo Park Presbyterian Church writes:

> Leaders of these programs have discovered they have a chance to minister to nonbelievers who fit the discouraged worker profile. People can go to many places to search for jobs. But they cannot always find the emotional support needed for the process. Of the average 110 attendees at Menlo Park's Saturday morning meetings, over a third are unchurched. Murata said, "It lifts their spirits. They understand that there is a framework or organization that can provide some of the emotional and spiritual pieces that are missing from secular job-seeking aid." For most people, a season of unemploy-

[24] https://partnerships.workforce3one.org/page/job_clubs (accessed Jan 14, 2012)

[25] Elissa, Cooper. Blessed are the Jobless: How Ministries Aid the Unemployed http://www.christianitytoday.com/ct/2012/january/, 2.

ment is temporary. If the church reaches out to nonbe-
lievers, they begin to grasp the difference between job
and vocation, which gives them a sense of God's direction and plan. "Where God puts us is not necessarily
where we want to be or where we think we should be,"
Veith said. "You would like to serve in a spectacular
way with everything going for you, but now you're doing something that you feel under-qualified for. Well,
this is where you're assigned. Serve *here*." That sense
of God-given call can motivate a discouraged worker to
move forward.[26]

The Church is usually quick and generous when responding to nat-
ural disasters. We see the physical devastation and the emotional
distress of those affected and we often respond. Many, if not most,
churches set about their work to minister to those who are broken
through family dysfunction, addictions, gangs, criminal behavior,
lack of proper nutrition, and even poor educational opportunities.
Someone would be hard-pressed to say the Church "doesn't care"
when it comes to stepping up and striving to strengthen the community in these areas.

However, for various reasons, unemployment doesn't look the same as
these other maladies. Its pathology is insidious. Emotional, psychological, and spiritual issues are masked by severance, unemployment "benefits," and the material possessions one has accumulated. Pervasive
unemployment isn't just a detriment to the individual, but it negatively
impacts the family, the immediate community, and society in general.
In our American culture, the societal struggle brought on by pervasive,
long-term unemployment may be the single greatest opportunity in the
last 50 years for the Church to live out its missional mandate. This opportunity will require leadership to think more holistically, a redistribu-
tion of the Church's resources, and the long-term efforts of the people
involved in the training, mentoring, and investing necessary to change
the employment landscape.

---

[26] Elissa, Cooper. Blessed are the Jobless: How Ministries Aid the Unemployed
http://www.christianitytoday.com/ct/2012/january/, 3.

WHAT NOW? *(Bud Searcy)*

What now? How do we take all of this information and translate it into some form of usable plan that will make a difference in the areas of unemployment and poverty in our city? The challenge can often seem overwhelming. As we have seen, the Christian community is actively engaged at various levels. However, the efforts are not nearly enough. What can the Church do to make a dent in this overwhelming problem? The answer can be found in the old adage, "How do you eat an elephant? One bite at a time."

PREPARING FOR RAIN *(Bud Searcy)*

In the film *Facing the Giants*, a story is told of two farmers that prayed for rain. However, only one of them prepared his fields to receive it. Which of the two had greater faith? The one who prepared his field, of course. In light of this, how do we "prepare our field" in Fresno to receive the blessing of God in the area of high unemployment in the context of high concentrated poverty? The following comments are mere suggestions that can get our thinking going in concrete ways.

First Suggestion: *Use this book as an educational resource.* Hopefully, we have been convinced by now that the line between the sacred and the secular is arbitrary at best. Work is part of what it means to be made in the image of God, and God is glorified in our work. It is nothing short of an act of love to help others find meaningful employment that enables them to provide for their families, gives them a sense of self-worth and purpose, and contributes to society. Therefore, creating ministries that generate jobs and that help people prepare for, find, and keep jobs is a spiritual endeavor in which the Church must engage. However, many churches and Christians do not see things from this frame of reference. Because of this, using this resource to lay a theological foundation is imperative. Christian leaders would do well to help their congregations grasp the larger implication of the Church's responsibility to the city in which they live with the following verses:

> *"When it goes well with the [uncompromisingly] righteous, the city rejoices...By the blessing of the influence*

of the upright and God's favor [because of them] the city is exalted" (Proverbs 11:10-11, Amplified Bible).

"And seek [inquire for, require, and request] the peace and welfare of the city to which I have caused you to be carried away captive; and pray to the Lord for it, for in the welfare of [the city in which you live] you will have welfare" (Jeremiah 29:7, Amplified Bible).

Second Suggestion: *Use this book to be encouraged by and informed about what Christian organizations are already doing locally, nationally, and abroad.* Some churches and cities are doing amazing things. We, too, must be willing to be creative and engage these issues in unorthodox ways. Think outside the four walls of your church or organization and be willing to do something new and innovative. Some of the examples in this book of what churches are doing in other areas can give us ideas of what we can potentially do in Fresno, if we are prayerful and willing to pursue something unique and daring. There is no reason that we in Fresno cannot duplicate or adapt to our area what has worked successfully elsewhere. If the church in Memphis has created Advance Memphis, why can't we adapt that concept to our area and create Advance Fresno? If Father Boyle of Los Angeles was able to take gang members off the streets of Los Angeles and make them productive members of society through Homeboy Industries, why can't we do something similar in our gang-impacted areas? And what if a number of Christian entrepreneurs and Christian organizations helped start businesses to employ and train the hard to employ or at-risk youth like Youth Industries in San Francisco, Christ Kitchen in Spokane Washington or Greystone Bakery in Yonkers?

Third Suggestion: *Look inwardly at the gifts, expertise, talents, and strengths of your own church.* Do an assessment of the gifts present in your congregation. This assessment must go beyond the usual spiritual gifts listed in Scripture. Within most congregations are experienced educators, business owners, entrepreneurs, accountants, computer techs, and more. Typically, there are also those who would be excellent mentors, job coaches, or vocational trainers. Whatever talent, gift, expertise, or strength we posses and yield to the Spirit of God to do His work can be used to transform people, neighborhoods, and communities. Discover your assets and capitalize on them.

Fourth Suggestion: *Be willing to work outside the four walls of your church in ways that make a difference with the unemployment and poverty problem in our community.* Far too many churches are only interested in ministering to their own. We can no longer afford to have this "business as usual" attitude in the face of our current crisis. We can no longer just *do* church. We must *be* the Church that is engaged in our community, working to make a difference.

As the Church scattered, Christians from every church throughout the city must be willing to volunteer their time. Organizations like the Fresno Rescue Mission, Samaritan Women, Evangel Home, Hope Now For Youth, Read Fresno, The Bridge Academy, and others are always in need of mentors, tutors, GED or literacy teachers, job coaches, computer teachers, and more. However, they never seem to have enough volunteers. While there are many reasons for this, a significant one is that too few people are willing to do long-term, sustaining ministry. If we are going to make a real difference, we must be willing to provide both long-term time and relational investments in the lives of those who are unemployed and stuck in poverty. Don't know where to volunteer or what opportunities are available? Organizations like the Fresno Rescue Mission offer tours that can help you determine where you best fit. Also, the volunteer website www.handsonnetwork.org offers a wide spectrum of organizations and volunteer opportunities.

As the Church gathered, identify the needs in the backyard of your church. Are there neighborhoods or apartment complexes with concentrated poverty? Is there a concentration of identifiable people groups? Are there signs of gang activity? Are there a lot of "For Sale" signs on homes in the area? In order to effectively minister to our respective communities, we must move from being "commuter churches" to becoming "community churches." In "commuter churches," people in middle class and wealthy neighborhoods come into a poor or declining area of town to attend church services and then return home, leaving the area surrounding the church untouched. In contrast, a "community church" invests in the surrounding community and, therefore, becomes the center of social activities, practical help, and services.

What can one church do to make a difference in the areas of unemployment and poverty? Only as much as our collective imagination can dream. What if there were church-based job fairs, support groups for the unemployed, computer training classes, GED or literacy classes, job readiness workshops, or job placement services? Some churches have already adopted schools in their area through Every Neighborhood Partnership and are involved in providing tutoring to children. However, many more schools need adopting. Other churches have adopted impoverished apartment complexes. What if volunteers from each church were available on-site to help children do their homework or to assist with resume development?

Christian organizations are now starting businesses that hire and train the hard to employ, as well as provide a source of income for the organization. Several local and national organizations are doing just that. The Fresno Rescue Mission, for example, has started a thrift store, is currently in the process of starting a for-profit janitorial service, and is looking to start other for-profit businesses in the future, all under a separate non-profit.

While these companies are hiring graduates of the program, they mainly act as vehicles for hands-on vocational training to prepare men and women to find jobs with other, similar companies or enable them to start their own business. In all of this, an indirect, but added bonus is that these endeavors could bring money into the organization. What would stop churches from doing something similar? Can you imagine the impact if 100 churches started for-profit businesses for the same purpose? Thousands of people once unemployed would join the workforce again. What if those who have started businesses held classes to teach others how to start their own businesses with little upfront costs?

The hard to employ will have difficulty finding employers willing to hire them due to felonies, few marketable skills, or sketchy work history. It is sad to see people who have turned their lives around from histories of drugs and prison return to lives of crime because no one was willing to give them jobs to enable them to support their families. For many of those, having or learning a skill that they can leverage into a legitimate business is the only hope they have of gainful, sustainable employment.

Fifth Suggestion: *Realize the power of partnerships, collaboration, and networking*. Today's version of unity is seen in partnerships, collaboration, and networking. We are better together, with church and non-profits working in unison towards a common goal of helping prepare people for and retain sustainable employment. With more, we can do more. With the sharing of resources and expenses, each organization can capitalize on its strengths, as well as resource and conjoin them with other organizations that also bring theirs to the equation. Churches must be willing to partner with other churches and non-profits in a way that looks past denominational differences or perceived competition between groups.

Many possible versions of this type of unified approach exist to tackle unemployment. Churches in a given area of the city can work together to reach the people in that particular area. Existing Pastor's Clusters can be a good place to start because relationships between Christian leaders have already been developed. Demographic study in a given area can identify key information regarding indigenous people groups and neighborhoods of concentrated poverty. In poorer areas of the city, larger churches with more resources could partner with these people groups and support more indigenous efforts by churches in that area.

Can you imagine a multi-campus vocational training center like the one described in the third chapter of this book? Hats off to Cornerstone Church's valiant effort! In that chapter, a valuable lesson was learned from its failed attempt:For programs of this nature to be sustainable, as well as be taken to scale, several congregations would most likely need to partner together in a collaborative effort that shared program costs, administration, facilities, leadership, and more. We might envision separate congregations throughout the city, each focusing on a different area of job training, linked together with other congregations doing a different area, utilizing a central administrative system and board. What a great idea: one vocational training center and many campuses! We already have a similar educational model called Fresno Christian Schools, which features one school and several sites.

Sixth Suggestion: *Don't ignore the hard to employ!* Who are the hard to employ? They are those with criminal backgrounds and felonies, the homeless, those from generational poverty, the welfare dependant, the addicted, gang members, the uneducated or undereducated, victims of sexual exploitation or trafficking, at-risk youth, the disabled, and immigrants, among others. In biblical times, most of these people would have been classified as "the poor." And, while God has immense love for us all, the poor occupy a special place in His heart. Most of these people are hard to employ due to years of addiction or jail and/or prison. They most likely have had handfuls of jobs, which they worked for only a few months, or they may have no work history at all. Some have few marketable skills, are high school drop-outs, or are illiterate. Some have many skills used in illegal business activities. Some are irresponsible and unreliable. Some can't seem to stay clean and sober for any length of time. This group is also the biggest drain on community resources and services.

For the greatest success in engaging this population, work with programs preparing them for the workforce. The participants in these programs are usually going through a process of becoming much more employable: recovery, personal transformation, job skills development, and job readiness. Several local organizations have good job readiness programs. Churches can also have job readiness programs to meet the needs of the people from that area of town. (You will find two good resources for job readiness curriculum at the end of this chapter.) Other local organizations may be using equally effective programs that can be implemented, as well.

An often-neglected piece in working with the hard to employ is the need for soft skills training. A person may have skills to get a job, but do they have the soft skills necessary to keep that job and succeed in the workplace? Employers are finding that too many people from the described groups lack work ethic and people skills necessary to succeed in the workplace. These workers fail to show up on time and ask for frequent time off to deal with personal problems. They create issues with coworkers and argue with supervisors over simple requests. They often leave jobs with little notice after only a few months, and before the employer has had any return on their investment in recruitment and training. This occurs, in part, because our increasingly diverse workforce brings varied beliefs and customs regarding appropriate behavior at work. The common sense expectations many employers hold may be foreign to those with little experience in the workplace.

The Academy at the Fresno Rescue Mission has chosen to implement "Workin' It Out," a soft skills training curriculum, into our existing job readiness program. This is a cognitive-behavioral program devised by Dr. Steve Parese that targets ex-offenders, at-risk youth, and those on welfare. This approach uses realistic stories, interactive role-playing, and thought-provoking activities to help participants better understanding the unspoken rules of the workplace. Participants also learn and practice useful skills for communicating and resolving common work-related problems. The Academy chose this program because of its proven track record (mostly in the Eastern and Midwestern United States) and its unique approach. Though the program is new, the Academy has already seen positive results. What if several churches and organizations currently or planning to do job readiness programs brought Dr. Parese to Fresno and each organization sent a representative to become a certified trainer in this soft skills approach?

Seventh Suggestion: *A call to Christian business people.* It is sad that an individual can go through a life-changing program, in which he or she becomes a different person, clean and sober, with restored relationships and job skills, and prepared to find a job, but no one will hire him or her because of the past. If he or she can't find a job, it is likely that that person will return to what is known in order to survive. I have seen this happen far too often during my time at the Academy.

A Christian business owner recently confessed to me that he had given little thought or prayer to how his faith impacts his business. God had been speaking to him and his fellow associates regarding offering a training opportunity for men with backgrounds that make them hard to employ in order to give them a chance at either advancing through the company or giving them the experience to find gainful employment with another company. When hired, that man would be matched with a mentor for the first six months of employment to increase the likelihood of success. What a great idea!

Thankfully, Fresno already has businesspeople that hire the hard to employ. Hope Now For Youth, The Academy, and Samaritan Women—to name a few—have employer friends that have experience hiring former gang members, felons, and recovering addicts. They have been willing to take a chance and have experienced both successes and failures. In all, they have learned important lessons along the way. However, there are not nearly enough employers willing to take that risk.

If a business owner is willing to consider hiring any of the described groups, I'd like to make three suggestions:

1. It's not recommended that you hire someone fresh off the streets. Instead, work through an organization.

2. Never offer someone a job if he or she is already in a program. Instead, communicate with the staff to discern the right timing.

3. Never hire someone that either left a program or was terminated. These are some of the reasons business owners who have hired the hard to employ have been burned and vowed to never hire anyone in a similar position again.

While there are no guarantees, I believe that following the above provides the best chance for success both for the employer and the employee.

CONCLUSION

Those of us working on this research project for the last six months have concluded that the status quo response to Fresno's unemployment crisis is actually quite dangerous. If we as God's people keep responding in the same way to the current crisis, we will create more of what we have already have: tremendous suffering in a growing sector of our populous and a militant detachment from a shrinking privileged sector. This is untenable, and the raw material for an explosion.

If the churches of Fresno fail to act, either Fresno will explode with even more violence, or it will simply wither and die a slow and painful death. If God's people in our city are to demonstrate the transforming power of the Gospel in our present circumstances, we must choose a proactive posture. We must choose involvement that may stretch us beyond what is comfortable in order to adopt forms that we might have initially thought were outside of the purview of the Church. However, the earth is the Lord's, right? So let's go to work.

SIX

An Invitation to the Edge:
A Director of a Non-Faith-Based Agency Reflects on the Role that Fresno's Faith Community Can Play to Prepare Our Low-Income Residents for Gainful and Sustainable Employment

By Paul McLain-Lugowski

The City of Fresno is fortunate to have a large, diverse, and vibrant faith community. This is important, given the intractable economic conditions of the Central Valley, exacerbated by a prolonged global recession. With other 4,000 non-profit agencies operating in our area and numerous government programs designed to assist those in need, the unique qualities of our faith community and its unrestricted mission to serve should be tapped.

The process of preparing anyone for sustainable employment at a living wage—with needed benefits—is extensive and cannot, nor should it be,contemplated in a vacuum. It can even be a difficult and lengthy process for those raised under the most favorable, stable, and supportive circumstances. Now, imagine the quest to become employable for anyone raised without the benefit of a stable home; loving parents; adequate, nutritious food; wholesome recreation; access to the arts; a safe neighborhood; and a variety of career role models.

Traditional employment preparation programs designed by our public institutions focus on inputs (i.e., structured classes, workshops, job shadowing, on-the-job training, etc.) and outcomes (i.e., a job, job retention, and wage growth). Programs tend to be relatively brief—from several weeks to a year in duration—and provide limited follow-up. Because most are funded on a competitive basis, should these programs fail to be funded during any particular cycle, or if funds are cut, the investment in an oft-elaborate infrastructure with a skilled, experienced staff may be compromised. At times, a particular, well-intended focus of a program—targeting offenders or persons in particular zip codes, for example—inadvertently overlooks others with needs just as great. And, of course, funding is never adequate to bring any program, even the best one, to scale, so we cannot depend exclusively on publicly funded solutions for any of our social or economic problems. Please don't misunderstand: there are many outstanding and proven publicly sponsored employment programs. Yet, the magnitude of our need for a well-trained, skilled workforce is simply more than any one system can provide.

However, the employment training challenge goes far beyond the capacity and quality of training providers. Imagine a single mother, without a high school diploma and without a vehicle. Though eager for training, her participation in a program, let alone a job, can be quite complicated. When her children become ill, who will care for them? Likely residing in rental housing, she and her family may unknowingly be exposed to home health hazards—lead, mold, radon, and more— all certain to have an impact on family health. Lacking a convenient grocery and knowledge of nutrition, the general health of her family and consequently her ability to meet attendance requirements, will be challenging. Bus service may not be available during the hours she needs to attend training or work, and bus service is not always reliable. Car pools may not be available. If she is fortunate to own a vehicle, it will not be reliable without costly, regular maintenance. That leaves cycling, or walking—both of which may be unrealistic, if not impossible, to get the single mother to her appointments. If she is involved in the justice system, there will be additional demands on her time. Court, parole, or probation appointments will cause absences not tolerated by employers. If she struggles with substance abuse or other dependency issues, it will be difficult for her to secure or retain employment. Job retention will also be jeopardized if she lacks a work ethic or the ability to relate properly to authority.

So, in the face of these deep challenges, what role can the faith community play to support the development of a qualified workforce? I believe the faith community of Fresno brings the following five *edges* to this conversation:

1. *Its edge*: The motivation of mission, love, and genuine concern—not time, money, prestige, or recognition.

2. *Its edge*: The willingness and *call* to live among the poor, in their neighborhoods, to be a light, a mentor, a friend, to provide a *hand up* for those desperate for help. To *roll up its sleeves* daily to provide attention, counsel, love, assistance, encouragement, and opportunity amid constant queries by curious children, youth seeking a caring coach and a safe place to play, and families eager for quality child care so they can seek employment.

3. *Its edge*: The freedom to count success by the number of people it touches each day, not by emails sent, meetings held, reports written, or documents processed.

4. *Its edge*: That its agenda, programs, goals, strategies, *are those of the people its serves.* Fundamentally, deliberately, and uncompromisingly *grassroots,* the faith community has an ability to grow indigenous leaders, knowing that lasting change and lasting improvement come about *only* when the community chooses, and in the way in which community leaders design and foster it. Programs come and go, organizations come and go, but leaders empower communities through broad investment in families.

5. *Its edge*: In the tradition of *barn raising,* it comprehends the incredible assets in our community and understands that the prosperous community is the community that creates trusting interaction, and mutual support so that the ensuing rising tide lifts all boats!

You may wonder what all this has to do with employment training, with job development, and with career exploration, yet *a solid personal, family, community foundation is necessary on which to build education and training, both of which lead to the skills employers seek today.*

A December 13, 2011 *Financial Times* article written by Hal Weitzman and Robin Harding is perceptively entitled "U.S. Companies Blame Unemployment on Skills Gap." Below are a few of their findings and insights:

- U.S. manufacturers have 600,000 unfilled positions because of a lack of qualified skilled workers, according to an October report released by Deloitte and the National Association of Manufacturers.

- Ben Bernanke, Chairman of the U.S. Federal Reserve, told an audience in Jackson Hole, Wyoming in August that the United States had to "foster the development of a skilled workforce" if it was to enjoy good, longer-term prospects. The U.S. education system, "despite considerable strengths, poorly serves a substantial portion of our population," he said.

- A September Kaufman Foundation poll of owners of fast-growing, privately held companies found that 40% of respondents said they were being held back by the skills gap, compared to just 13% by lack of demand (for workers).

- American 15-year-olds ranked 25th among the 34 developed countries in the Organization for Economic Cooperation and Development (OECD) in math, 17th in science, and 14th in reading ability, according to a 2009 OECD study.

I conclude from these findings and from years of personal experience in this field that the faith community is today in greater demand than ever. I think we all agree that *the substance of faith is rooted in expressions of genuine care and compassion for our fellow humans and results in the restoration of justice and the sharing of our abundance, our skills, talents, and resources so that all—even the weakest among us—responsibly participate, to the extent they are able, to seek the prosperity of the community.* Along the way, we must celebrate movements in this direction, such as:

- The youth, first in his family to graduate from high school!

- The alley, safe now for children to walk through to school!

- The street corner with a volunteer crossing patrol, instead of a drug dealer!

- The community garden raising healthy, nutritious vegetables, to raise a healthy, new generation!

- The grandfather reading to his grandchild on the porch, no longer fearful of bullet spray!

- The playground now populated with screaming children, screaming for the winning shot rather than the thunder of nearby gunfire!

- The father, mother, son, and daughter tired from a full day's work, no longer tired of constant collection notices!

- The youth pumping a fist with exhilaration having opened a college admissions letter, instead of a notice from a probation officer!

- The budding entrepreneur having just opened a new storefront for business, removing the plywood that once covered the abandoned building!

And, the smile on the family's face with keys to a new home in hand, the same family that once called a secluded overpass home!

These are the benchmarks and the context in which progress toward employment and career development will be made. Now, it's time to *roll up our sleeves*.

EPILOGUE

Commencement Address from the Year 2035

By Mayor Pa Hua Vang
(fictitious)

To the Fresno Pacific University Class of 2035:

You may not believe this, but the city in which you now live and love, the one you brag about with your friends in Los Angeles and San Francisco, the one attracting so many airlines that we just had to finish another terminal—well, that city didn't exist just 23 years ago when you were born. You take it for granted that this beautiful city has always been the envy of the state, but it hasn't. You don't remember the day when Fresno was listed as the least desirable place to live in the nation. It's hard to fathom how we tolerated so much that was so wrong for so long. But now, what a transformation! The contrast between then and now is astounding.

If you don't believe me, just ask your parents about 2015. Fresno had become known as the car-theft capital of California. We suffered from chronic 17% unemployment. The number of illegal businesses and corner vending had skyrocketed, depriving the city of needed tax increment and preventing it from repairing anything. Seemed like graffiti covered almost every surface. The high school dropout rate was something like 60%. Yearly reports reminded us of our concentrated poverty. And even worse than these individual hardships: somehow we had slipped into thinking that that was our lot, that somehow we had been dealt an inevitable and impossible hand. Aside from a few rabble-rousers, most folks had just accepted all those things as unchangeable.

And then, over just a few short years, almost as from a bad dream, we woke up—slowly, at first—and decided that it didn't have to be that way. So, what happened? Let me see if I can describe it.

WHAT HAPPENED?

Some of us remember that, in 2015, after some half-hearted attempts at putting bandages on the problems, a new spirit of innovation began to grip the faith community: the churches, and non-profit ministries of our city. We tried a few things, and those led to bigger things, and—low-and-behold—actual solutions began to emerge. We sort of looked at each other across a few churches and said, "Whoa, that worked." At first, it was just an idea that followers of Christ would see the transformation of their city as an integral expression of their faith. Out of that kind of thinking, specific plans emerged.

I remember having to work through a few failures that threatened to plunge us back into cynicism. We held some huge food giveaways, which always made us feel good, but that feeling tended to fade when we saw longer lines the following year. We created housing solutions for a few hundred homeless people, but the word got out, and Fresno became a magnet for homeless from around the state. We couldn't keep up, and our streets ended up worse than before. A church tried to do a vocational school, but couldn't sustain it by itself.

CARS

However, over the first few years of trying new things, we saw some modest successes. For example, with regard to car thefts, community groups began to work with the police department, school principals, pastors, and local businesses in an innovative program that targeted first-time offenders and got them placed with a victim-offender mediator, an initial vocational training course paid for by local industry, and life-skills courses offered by churches that had scholarships attached to them for vocational schools or community colleges. Eventually, 400 of the 500 churches in Fresno participated, writing these scholarships into their congregational budgets and the courses into their church schedules. Car thefts gradually started to drop off, but then dramatically fell after that, as youth saw a pathway out of their circumstances.

BUSINESS COACHES

However, it didn't end there. Churches were so encouraged by the results that several of them banded together to pay for a small business facilitator. This coach worked with churches to identify people in their congregations who had the dream of starting a small business, but not the necessary experience to develop and monitor a business plan nor the capital to begin. The facilitator ran monthly workshops using church facilities in every part of the city, and provided guidance for navigating the ins and out of becoming a legal business. It seemed like these workshops were sparsely attended at first, as people weren't sure that a church could do this. It was, in fact, a little out of the box.

Gradually, however, people started participating as the facilitator also coordinated the already existing small business incubators and other governmental agencies so that congregational members could learn the process and take full advantage of what was already there. The facilitator also offered financial literacy seminars for members. These turned out to be hugely successful, as the Gospel remained at the center of their curriculum. Annual seminars were also started for the pastoral community so it would thoroughly understand how to resource the Body.

I'll never forget when the mayor's office called to tell us that the number of applications for new business permits doubled that first year. They couldn't contain themselves. The number tripled each year after that, and the city began to see improvement in its available budget. I remember lots of churches gathering residents to hear what they needed repaired in their communities, and the city was able to create a game plan based on their input. They spent the new tax increment on improving infrastructure. Fresno's physical environment began to shine after a few years, almost as brightly as its citizens did. Even downtown! None of us could believe it when Macy's wanted to renovate on of the old stores on the Fulton Mall. That was a signal that we had entered a new era.

CHURCH-BASED VOCATIONAL SCHOOLS

In one of the more interesting developments, and partly catalyzed by the small business facilitator, ten churches created a vocational school together, which they ran using church facilities at four different ethnic-specific areas in the city, including African American, Hmong & Lao, Mexican, and White. Each campus offered a different skill, ranging from culinary arts, auto repair, medical billing, janitorial and cleaning, web development, and other areas. Hundreds of residents began to benefit each year, many gaining employment with established firms, and others starting their own businesses. Since these churches centralized administration and shared costs, it was sustainable. The Gospel also remained central to the success of these courses, since life issues were dealt with spiritually, dealing directly with the barriers to employment with which so many struggled. There must be 2,000 people per year being trained in that system now. Imagine that: it only took ten of Fresno's 500 churches to provide a solution for 5% of Fresno's most vulnerable people.

INDIVIDUALIZED DEVELOPMENT ACCOUNTS

With the momentum continuing to build, more than 100 churches signed up and got the training for managing Individualized Development Accounts (IDAs), which trained people to save even small amounts, which were then matched—sometimes up to the power of 7 to 1—by grants: some private, some from church budgets, and some public. People used them for things like vocational training, equipment for businesses, increasing inventory, or just as savings. These were a powerful catalyst, and a newly invigorated small business community became responsible for a new economic renaissance in Fresno. We no longer waited for large corporations to come and solve our economic woes. Interestingly, as these accounts sparked more business, churches found that recipients were tithing on their gains and, in turn, strengthening the outreach of the church in town.

JESUS DELIVERS

A former delivery driver and several construction and service companies with a Kingdom focus saw potential opportunity and imagined what they could achieve together through teamwork. With the goal of getting the right product delivered to the right location, they created a company that could employ individuals who only had experience with physical labor. At first, churches donated vans. Then, a Christian CEO at a local delivery firm donated several trucks when his company upgraded.

This gave birth to Shalom Logistics, which quickly grew. It began delivering for thrift stores, construction sites, furniture businesses, and grocery stores until over 1,000 companies were using their services—keeping profitability, jobs, and income from Sanger to Aubery in motion. Through this effort, over 200 jobs have been provided for residents of Fresno County. Employees routinely gather for prayer, and employees have started celebrating "God solutions" to common problems, both at work and in their personal lives. They provide a better service to companies, all the while allowing the original businesses to focus on their targeted industries and successfully grow.

KNOCK ON WOOD

A group of Christians in construction and related industries in Fresno found woodworking and cabinet building businesses were adversely affected when, in 2008, construction jobs nearly evaporated. Many skilled workers were out of work, and many more roofers and rough construction workers, too. Utilizing resources and equipment that had been set aside and were collecting dust, they formed a business creating local, customized furniture. Marketed in churches as a "hand up," not a "hand out," these beds incorporated carved scenes from Fresno, Yosemite, Sequoia, and the Central Coast, and became wildly popular. Purchasing directly from their shop kept overhead costs lower, benefiting the company, as well as their customers. Nearly 100 new jobs were created initially, and they have now expanded. The City of Fresno was in need of new office furniture and hired this furniture company to outfit the City Hall. It was enriching for them to be able to visit the factory and meet the crews creating their furniture. The vision has caught on and the company is packaging and delivering their furniture nationwide. It's amazing what can happen when skills and assets are utilized to their God-intended potential.

NOTHING STOPS A BULLET LIKE A BOOK

Another feature of Fresno's renaissance was that 300 of Fresno's 500 churches adopted nearly 90% of all elementary schools in Fresno, with church members providing tutoring and mentoring for something like 80% of all children in the school district. Schools were overwhelmed with support. This, more than any other factor, overcame the terrible dropout rate and, though no could have guessed this was possible back then, now Fresno shines as the premier example of educational perseverance in California. That was a remarkable accomplishment in itself. However, the other byproduct was that, year after year, those children continued their success and went onto college or vocational school more than at any time in our history. The outcome of this included the attraction of major corporations to Fresno because of its educated workforce—both in white-collar and blue-collar workers. Success has bred success.

GETTING THE FACTS STRAIGHT

One of the tipping points in our transformation happened when the city's local Christian university became a large player as a data management research engine. Its facilitation in the citywide Learn2Earn program helped track the progress of vulnerable people who chose to take an onramp toward greater education. This allowed them to see the "big picture" of who our local CBOs were serving and where they were being served. With that info, the school could help these CBOs better serve families in a holistic manner, with each organization serving a specialty, thus allowing a sister organization to serve in a different area.

This unity in organizational services and data management allowed Fresno to become a leader in service industries, as well as financial resources. State and government funding began to flow in easily as Fresno became known as a united entity of CBOs. There was no over-duplication of services, everyone shared their data, outcomes were easier to see, and there was never a sense of "competition" between leaders.

SOFT SKILLS FOR HARD TIMES

It wasn't just youth that were on the road to educational success. Churches and non-profits collaborated on soft skills training for people with significant barriers to employment, including the formerly incarcerated. At one point, a wave of nearly 40,000 inmates were released from California prisons due to overcrowding, but churches and non-profits were ready for them with training for every one, helping them with resume writing, interviewing, work-skills, respecting authority, and more. The police noted publically how they had expected crime to go up when the inmates were released, but everyone was amazed when it didn't. The old adage "Nothing stops a bullet like a job" came home clearly to us during that time.

A CULTURAL RENAISSANCE

What started as a simple art class at a local church 15 years ago for youth slowly rippled into a citywide church movement to feature and develop music, dance, and the visual arts in our city. Neighborhood churches added venues to the popular "Art Hop" evenings. This led to the Fresno Institute of the Arts—a place you know to have an international reputation as a center focused on the educating of individuals whose talents can be developed and directed toward the shalom of their own cities. This turned out to be an economic boon for Fresno and our region, as artists throughout the region descended on our city to experience this supportive atmosphere. This led to the artistic revival that you know today, birthing a myriad of dance academies, music studios, and a host of new galleries.

A NEW FRESNO

Around the year 2020, it began to dawn on us as the employment picture steadily improved that our civic vision was improving, as well. Green projects and public art began to pop up everywhere, and Fresno won a national award for the most trees planted in any city. Articles in the *Los Angeles Times* and the *San Francisco Chronicle* started to take notice of Fresno's desirability. Just last year, in the October 2034 edition, *TIME Magazine* did a feature on Fresno, listing it as the "most transformed city in the U.S." Perhaps most significant of all, however: we now hear our own people talk about what a good place Fresno has become.

CONCLUSION

It's amazing to think that just a few churches and agencies decided to collaborate way back in 2015 and sparked this transformation. It was a joy to behold when the idea began to infect the entire faith community in the city. It's equally amazing these days to constantly hear Christians in Fresno remind each other to never let ourselves fall into passivity toward and separation from the problems of our city. As James writes, "Faith without works is dead." "When the righteous succeed, a city rejoices," as Proverbs reminds us. Perhaps most significantly, however, is that the future-oriented promise in Jeremiah has now become past tense for us: We sought the well being of Fresno, and we prayed to the Lord on its behalf. When we sought its well being, we found our own well being (Jeremiah 29:7, paraphrased, re-tensed).

So, graduates, it's time to take your place in a renewed city. We dare not slack off. Find your place in seeking the peace of Fresno.

APPENDIX A

Further Resources

BOOKS & ARTICLES

Article: "Blessed are the Jobless" by Elissa Cooper, *Christianity Today*, January 2012, pp. 32-34.

Business as Mission by C. Neal Johnson (IVP, 2009)

Business StartUP Training by Michael Clargo (the General Guide designed for churches available through tbnetwork.org)

Fighting Poverty Through Social Enterprise: The Case for Social Venture Capital, by Brian Griffiths and Kim Tan (Alden Press, UK, 2007)

Future Profits: Financial Literacy and Life Skills Education by Northern California Urban Development (www.ncud.org)

Gangs to Jobs, by Roger Minassian (Alpha Publishing, 2003)

How to Change the World: Social Entrepreneurs and the Power of New Ideas, by David Bornstein (Oxford University Press, 2004)

Job Shadowing Daniel: Walking the Talk at Work by Larry Peabody (Outskirts Press, 2010)

Spiritual Enterprise: Doing Virtuous Business, by Theodore Malloch (Encounter Books, 2008)

Starting Up Now: 24 Steps to Launch Your Own Business, by L. Brian Jenkins (StartingUp Business Solutions, 2011)

Tattoos on the Heart, by Father Gregory Boyle (Free Press/Simon & Schuster, 2010)

The Other Six Days: Vocation, Work and Ministry in Biblical Perspective, by R. Paul Stevens (Eerdmans, 2000)

Think and Act Anew: How Poverty in American Affects Us All and What We Can Do About It, by Larry Snyder (Orbis Books, 2010)

Work: A Kingdom Perspective on Labor, by Ben Witherington (Eerdmans, 2011)

Merchant to Romania, by Jeri Little, Day One Publications, 2009

IDEAS & STRUCTURES

Job Clubs: Designed for individuals who coordinate, facilitate, or participate in local job clubs at a religious institution, community center, or even online, job clubs play an important role in helping unemployed community members find a new job and manage the challenges associated with unemployment. Learn how to start or sustain your job club, connect to the local public workforce system, network with other job club coordinators, and share your own experiences and best practices. Get lists of churches and agencies that are doing job clubs in your state. To learn more, please visit www.DOL.gov/jobclubs.

VIDEOS

Ten9Eight: Shoot for the Moon: A video by Mary Mazzio, featuring stories of inner city teens in entrepreneurial training.

Jobs for Life: Flip the List: Epipheo Studios
   (www.youtube.com/user/Jobs4Life)

ASSOCIATIONS AND WEBSITES

The Network for Teaching Entrepreneurship (www.NTFE.com)

The Transformational Business Network (www.tbnetwork.org)

Jobs For Life (www.jobsforlife.org)Faith Venture Forum
   (www.faithventureforum.org)

The No Name Fellowship (www.nonamefellowship.com)

CURRICULUM

Workin' It Out
SOFT SKILLS TRAINING
Dr. Steve Parese
(336) 593-3533
www.WorkinItOut.com

Jobs For Life
www.jobsforlife.org

APPENDIX B

Local and National Non-Faith-Rooted
Job Readiness/Employment Programs or Entities

Association of Community Employment Programs (ACE)

New York City, New York
www.acenewyork.org

In 1992, Henry Buhl offered a homeless man a paid job of sweeping the sidewalk in front of his house, rather than just giving him money. Buhl challenged the neighbors and businesses on his block to do the same. Within months, word spread, and the non-profit was born. Today, ACE networks five boroughs of New York through Project Comeback and Project Stay—intensive and comprehensive programs with the aim of helping the homeless overcome barriers to employment, become employed, and maintain those jobs. These aims are accomplished through vocational training, on-the-job application, counseling and coaching, and a "life-long support network" for self-sufficiency. Project Comeback includes a stipend for the 20 hours of work each week cleaning streets and sidewalks. Project Stay rewards participants with financial incentives for Project Comeback graduates who meet employment and retention goals in permanent jobs. ACE is supported by private donors and foundations.

EOC Youth Build

YouthBuild Fresno
1805 E. California Ave.
Fresno, CA 93706
(559) 264-1048
lcc@fresnoeoc.org

Target Population: Young adults, ages 18-24, needing to complete their high school educationParticipants of the program work toward their diploma or GED while learning job skills by building or refurbishing low-income houses, performing landscaping, community clean-up, and more. YouthBuild Fresno provides:

- Quality, hands-on construction training

- Classroom instruction leading to a high school diploma

- Vocational computer training

- Up to $4,700 awarded to be used for continuing education

- Opportunities to improve the community

- Supportive services

- Assistance in finding and keeping a job

- Opportunities for leadership development

Goodwill Industries

Melissa Jahnke
mjahnke@goodwill-sjv.org
(209) 466-2311, ext. 202

Do you need a job, but don't think you have the right skills? Do you already have skills, but can't find the right job for you? That's where Goodwill can help. We provide job training and placement services to help you build the skills you need to get started on your way to a life-long career.

Helping Others Pursue Excellence (HOPE Build)

Laneesha Senegal
(559) 790-0993
Target Population: Young adults, 18-24 years oldAt HOPE Build, youth are trained in the simple trades of carpentry, plumbing, electrical, and more. There is also an entrepreneurial training course for youth hoping to begin their own businesses.

Proteus

Fresno Service Center
1815 Van Ness
Fresno, CA 93271
(559) 499-2140

Proteus offers counseling, English as a Second Language (ESL), career exploration, adult basic education, job-related educated, General Education Development (GED), vocational education, job search skills classes, on-the-job training, referrals, job placement, and supportive services. Some services may not be available in all offices. All Proteus services are free of charge. **SparkPoint (United Way)**

For more information, please dial 2-1-1 or send a message to sparkpoint@unitedwayfresno.org

This is a family-friendly place where hard-working, low- to moderate- income people can access a full range of services to help them get out of poverty and achieve long-term financial stability. SparkPoint Fresno Center brings together the most effective nonprofit and government partners to help clients build assets, grow income, and manage debt. SparkPoint clients work with a coach, who helps create a step-by-step plan to set and achieve personal financial goals. Because change does not happen overnight, SparkPoint commits to working with clients for up to three years to achieve their financial goals.

Workforce Connection

Manchester Center Mall
Arthur Moss
3302 N. Blackstone Avenue, Suite 155
Fresno, CA 93726
Telephone: (559) 230-3600
Fax: (559) 230-4022
amoss@workforce-connection.com
Hours of operation: Monday - Friday 8am - 5pm

Workforce Pipeline, a program of the East Baltimore Development Initiative (EBDI)

Baltimore, Maryland
www.ebdi.org

In 2003, this non-profit organization began its "case management model of family services" and development in the East Baltimore community, home of Johns Hopkins Hospital and Johns Hopkins University. The organization's many development projects, initiatives, and programs include Workforce Pipeline, whose goal is "empowering residents through employment and training." Workforce Pipeline offers job referrals, job readiness assessments and training, various industry training and apprenticeships, and job placements within EBDI's development projects and partner employers, for residents of East Baltimore.

Greyston Bakery

Yonkers, New York
www.greystonbakery.com

With the slogan "We don't hire people to bake brownies. We bake brownies to hire people," Greyston Bakery is a full-fledged bakery catering to high-end restaurants and events, and also ships goods via its online shop. Since 1982, the bakery has grown into a business employing an average of 65 people, all of whom were considered hard to employ. Many employees are referred directly, coming out of prison or drug and alcohol rehabilitation programs. New employees enter the bakery's apprenticeship, where they perform the monotonous work of the bakery, learning basic job skills on the job, while also earning the opportunity to become a paid employee of Greyston Bakery. During their apprenticeship, employees are also paired with a counselor who gives training, resourcing, and support to the employee to help him or her become self-sustaining. Those who become permanent employees are paid a living wage and receive benefits, wage increases, and promotions. For many employees, the bakery is a first step in gaining permanent employment with another employer. Former Director Julius Wolves says the bakery has a double bottom line: that the social mission is just as important as the business mission.

Greyston Bakery is a for-profit business, but its social mission goes beyond employment. The bakery also supports Greyston Foundation, which, among many other services, runs a childcare center, creates affordable housing, offers counseling services, and gives college scholarships. One of the accountants at Greyston Bakery tells of how she became homeless when she was 15 and dropped out of school. A few years later, she began standing in line every Wednesday at the bakery for its open hiring day. Finally, the day came when they had an opening, and she joined the apprenticeship. She took full advantage of the support offered, and eventually became self-supporting.

Sari Bari

West Bengal, India with corporate headquarters in *Omaha, Nebraska*
www.saribari.com

Sari Bari rescues women from the sex trafficking industry in India by providing a home, family environment, and employment on two sites located within red light districts. The women create various home decor goods and accessories sold through their online store. Because women are often sold into the commercial sex trade in order to provide for an impoverished family, Sari Bari also has two village sites to provide jobs for women as a prevention and alternative opportunity for women.

Delancey Street Foundation

San Francisco, California
www.delanceystreetfoundation.org

Founded in 1971 as a residential community for people seeking rehabilitation from drug addiction in San Francisco, Delancey Street Foundation now has combined vocational and residential programs in five cities throughout the United States. The average participant in Delancey Street "has been a hardcore drug and alcohol abuser, has been in prison, is unskilled, is functionally illiterate, and has a personal history of violence and generational poverty." Academics and vocational training are essential components to the comprehensive rehabilitation process. This is largely addressed through the 12 business enterprises developed through Delancey Street's vision of social entrepreneurship. "Economic development and entrepreneurial boldness are central to our model's financial self-sufficiency and to teaching residents self-reliance and life skills". The vocational and residential program is comprehensive, with a stay of 2 to 4 years. In the Foundation's forty years of service, they have graduated "over 18,000 people...into society as successful, taxpaying citizens leading decent, legitimate and productive lives."

Workforce Pipeline, a program of the East Baltimore Development Initiative

Baltimore, Maryland
www.ebdi.org

YouthBuild U.S.A.

www.youthbuild.org

YouthBuild is a federal program sponsored by community and faith-rooted non-profit organizations in 273 different communities nationwide. While programs may vary, the basic aim of YouthBuild is to serve youth, ages 16 through 24, with opportunities to complete their high school education and learn construction skills through training and on the job. YouthBuild builds affordable housing for low-income people in their communities.

New Door Ventures

San Francisco, CA
www.newdoor.org

New Door Ventures is a non-profit serving at-risk youth and young adults in San Francisco with educational support, job skills training, employment in its non-profit businesses, and placement in paid internships in its numerous business partnerships, all in a supportive environment.

Fresno County Library Literacy Services

www.fresnolibrary.org

For free tutor training for adults in GED or literacy, as well as free teaching materials, please contact Rebecca Wade at (559) 224-7094.

CONTRIBUTOR BIOGRAPHIES

Bryan Feil is the Director at Neighborhood Thrift. He is a FIFUL board member and Pink House alum. He graduated from Fresno State with a degree in Business and is married to his lovely wife, Kim. Email: bryan@neighborhoodthrift.com

Rev. Bud Searcy is currently the Director of the Academy Rehabilitation Program For Men at the Fresno Rescue Mission, a position he has held since 2003. Before that, he was the Executive Director for New Creation Ministries in Fresno for 17 years and was on staff at Valley Christian Center for five years. He is a graduate of Fresno Pacific University and has his Master's Degree in New Testament Studies, along with a minor in Pastoral Care and Counseling, from the Mennonite Brethren Biblical Seminary.

Rev. Dr. Randy White leads a global Doctoral Degree Program focused on training leaders from 39 countries for community transformation, and is the founder of IVCF's Fresno Institute for Urban Leadership (FIFUL). He is the author of *Encounter God in the City: Onramps to Personal and Community Transformation* (IVP, 2006) as well as many other books and articles on urban mission.

Kristi Nichols is the Work Experience Coordinator at Neighborhood Thrift. Prior to moving to Fresno in 1999, she served with InnerChange, an Order Among the Poor in Santa Ana and San Francisco for twelve years. She is married to John, a teacher and coach at Sunnyside High School, and has two children.

Rev. Dr. Jeffrey Craig Harrington has been a youth pastor, a church planter and is currently an Associate Pastor at New Harvest Church in Clovis, CA and the Executive Director of Highway City Community Development in Fresno. He earned a Masters in Christian Ministry from the Mennonite Brethren Biblical Seminary and a Doctorate of Ministry in Transformational Leadership from Bakke Graduate University. Before meeting Christ at the age of 30, he also obtained a Bachelor's in Business Administration from Fresno State. He is an adjunct professor at Fresno Pacific University and teaches Spiritual Formation and Ministry across Cultures in the degree completion program.

Artie Padilla is the director of Every Neighborhood Partnership, a Fresno community benefit organization that mobilizes local churches to serve surrounding elementary schools and neighborhoods. His call is to assist in unleashing the vast resources within the Body of Christ for the service of His Kingdom.

Paul McLain-Lugowski is Associate Executive Director for the Fresno County Economic Opportunities Commission (EOC), as well as founder and, for 17 years, Director of the EOC's Local Conservation Corps. Paul is a seminary graduate, and former local pastor.

Rev. Dr. Sharon Stanley is a passionate advocate for refugees and multi-cultural justice, is founder and Executive Director of Fresno Interdenominational Refugee Ministries that builds communities of hope with new Americans. She lived for 13 years in a Fresno slum named after a refugee camp in Thailand, and holds Doctor of Ministry and Master of Divinity degrees.